NOT READY FOR MARRIAGE, NOT READY FOR SEX:

ONE COUPLE'S RETURN TO CHASTITY

Chris and Linda Padgett

SERVANT BOOKS

PUBLISHED BY ST. ANTHONY MESSENGER PRESS
CINCINNATI, OHIO

Scripture passages have been taken from *New Revised Standard Version Bible*, copyright ©1989 by the Division of Christian Education of the National Council of the Churches of Christ in the U.S.A., and used by permission. All rights reserved. Quotations from *Catechism of the Catholic Church* are taken from the second edition of the English translation, copyright ©1997 by Libreria Editrice Vaticana, Citta del Vaticano.

Cover design by Cristina Mershon
Cover photo © Corbis
Book design by Mark Sullivan

Library of Congress Cataloging-in-Publication Data

   Padgett, Chris, 1970-
    Not ready for marriage, not ready for sex : one couple's return to
   chastity / Chris and Linda Padgett.
     p. cm.
   Includes bibliographical references.
   ISBN-13: 978-0-86716-745-0 (pbk. : alk. paper)
   ISBN-10: 0-86716-745-9 (pbk. : alk. paper)
   1. Chastity. 2. Catholic youth—Religious life. 3. Sex—Religious
   Aspects—Catholic Church. 4. Padgett, Chris, 1970- —Sexual
   behavior. 5. Padgett, Chris, 1970- —Sexual behavior. I. Padgett,
   Linda, 1970- . II. Title.
   BV4647.C5P33 2006
   241'.66—dc22

                     2005037098

ISBN-13: 978-0-86716-745-0
ISBN-10: 0-86716-745-9

Published by Servant Books, an imprint of St. Anthony Messenger Press.
28 W. Liberty St.
Cincinnati, OH 45202
www.AmericanCatholic.org

Printed in the United States of America.
Printed on acid-free paper.
06 07 08 09 10 5 4 3 2 1

Contents

Preface

Hey, let's talk about sex! We were young and single once, so we know that sex rates right up there as one of your favorite subjects. Perhaps you're curious about sex and have a ton of questions and nobody with whom you're comfortable discussing this hot issue. Too often Christians treat sex as a taboo topic, not appropriate for open discussion. The only words of wisdom many adults offer young Christians are "Don't do it, and that's final!"

Well, we believe it's important to talk about sex. The silence and misinformation are not helping anyone. Some of you are willing to give up your virginity simply to be loved by someone right now. Some of you give yourselves to sexual intimacy because you want to understand what all the excitement is about.

Many people want to avoid the dreaded label *virgin*. After all, what could be worse? Well, HIV, AIDS and other sexually transmitted diseases (STDs) and, of course, the spiritual calamity that sex outside of marriage brings into your life. But we'll talk about all that later.

God gave us sex as a sacramental gift in which each partner selflessly gives himself or herself to the other, freely, permanently, exclusively, without fear and with openness to the possibility of creating new life. God wants his creation to multiply and have a good time doing it. Yet, just like other exceptional blessings and gifts, this one also needs to be protected and cherished.

Let's pretend your parents gave you a brand new sports car (we're dreaming big here). You wouldn't let just anyone drive it around town. You would treat that vehicle as one of your most prized possessions. Sex is a far greater gift, but unless it is protected and cherished and used as God intended—within marriage—it can lead to broken hearts and homes.

Far too many people treat this prized possession haphazardly. We were one such careless couple. We regularly abused this beautiful gift, using it for our own selfish purposes instead of trusting God for his perfect design in our lives. We messed up—*a lot*. Yet we were able to overcome the stronghold of promiscuity and turn our relationship into one that was pleasing to him.

So what about you? Do you feel ensnared by sexual activity? Does it seem as if all your efforts to do the right thing collapse the moment you are alone with your date? Are you trapped in the grip of sin, with no hope of victory? Do you wonder if God could possibly want you to serve him after all the mistakes you've made? Still worrying that your relationship will fall to pieces if you stop having sex?

This book contains a message for you. It is a story about a God who is bigger than your sins, mistakes, compromises and addictions. Not only can you have victory in your dating relationships, but you also can honor Christ in them. In making Jesus the center of your relationships, you open yourselves up to his unfolding plan of love for your life.

This is our story, one that, in terms of sexual promiscuity, is far too typical these days. We share how our early dating progressed into a desperate mess, how we moved from promiscuity to chastity and how we maintained that chastity for over two years before getting married.

The story we share is deeply personal; in fact, we've never told some parts of it to another living soul. So why are we putting it in a book for lots of people to read? We hope that our mistakes will warn you, that our experiences will encourage and convict you and that the topics we address will answer some of those troublesome questions you now face.

We pray that your current and future interactions with the opposite sex will be a safe place to discern a marriage or religious vocation. One last thought: let your dating relationships be models for younger siblings, so they can know how to treat the opposite sex when it is their time to date.

Dear reader, your next move is to turn the page and enter into our interesting and, at times, zany story. So buckle up and hang on. This may be one of the most adventurous reads of your life.

Acknowledgments

From Chris:

To Linda, my life-mate: We have grown up together, and you are my better half. I am still in love with you. Thanks for giving a goofy guy like me the time of day.

To Hannah, Sarah, Madeline, Noah, Kolbe, Mary, Jude and future little Padgetts: You are the fruit of your parents' love. You are the gifts God has blessed us with; we would not be who we've become without you. Thank you for every moment.

To Mom: You are my hero.

To Dad: You are my friend.

From Linda:

I dedicate this book to the three strengths in my life: the Lord Jesus, who calls me and enables me; my husband, who encourages, loves and trusts me; and my eight children, thus far, who are gems of joy

I also thank my mother for her prayers and sacrifice to produce in me the greatest gift of all—faith.

From both of us:

We would like to thank our spiritual leaders, both past and present, especially Father John, Father Girard, Father Augustine and Mark and Beth Miravalle.

We are grateful to those who have given us a model of Christian love, marriage and family life. These include many families in Steubenville, Ohio, but especially the Adams, Ferris, Hostetler, Sirillas, Sandford and Dombrowski families.

Thanks also to Cynthia Cavnar for her editorial guidance and to all those at Servant Books and St. Anthony Messenger Press who helped make this book a reality.

How to Make Sense of This Book

This book is laid out according to the natural way our relationship progressed. Each of the four sections tells a part of our story.

Section one, "Initial Infatuation," tells about our first two weeks together, from our meeting to the memorable first date.

Section two, "The Fall," moves into the struggles and conflicts that arose when we added sexual activity to our relationship.

In section three, "The Change," we share how our relationship moved from being sexually driven to spiritually focused. This is the victorious part of our journey.

Throughout these three sections we offer answers to questions we suspect are coming up in your mind. At the end of each of these sections we recommend that you write in a personal journal your insights as well as answers to specific questions that we pose.

Section four, "Hard Questions," deals with some difficult issues you and your friends may be facing, from conquering temptation to discerning God's call in your life. There we use our experience, Scripture, church teaching and the best advice we can find to address these concerns.

The epilogue was written to stir your thinking about how our experiences can inform your future decisions and actions in this spiritually important area of your life.

Appendixes A–C offer some further serious and not-so-serious information we want to share, and Appendix D guides you to additional on-topic reading material.

Though our dating experience had its sinful aspects, there are many wonderful moments of getting to know one another that we share under the title "Memory Moment." We also include some dating tips that might be helpful in your own relationships as well as "Padgett's Ponderings," occasional side-trips into Chris's mysterious brain.

So have fun, and may God bless you as you read.

SECTION ONE

INITIAL INFATUATION

A MOST UNIQUE PERSONALITY: LINDA MEETS CHRIS

As the first semester of senior year came to a close and Christmas approached, the students at Bayshore High School in Bradenton, Florida, became increasingly distracted. My friend Darci and I were no exception.

In an effort to forget the looming midterm exams, we chatted about the outcome of the "senior superlatives." This is a school tradition in which the seniors vote for those students they consider to be the best looking, most likely to succeed, most talented, to name a few. As we walked through the musty hallways of the aging building, heading to the overcrowded cafeteria, my cheerleading companion told me who the winners were.

A guy named Chris Padgett had won in the category of most unique personality of the senior class. "Who could this guy be?" I wondered. I thought I knew, or knew of, all the students in my class, but I had never heard of him.

"Oh, he moved here last year," Darci said. "He's very funny; he deserves to win." She explained that Chris was notorious for his extreme fashion and unpredictable conduct. For instance, he would trip intentionally and throw a stack of books all over the ground. His clothes were usually outrageously out of style and yet comically appealing.

We arrived at the cafeteria, which smelled, as usual, like a mixture of the daily special (your guess is as good as mine) and dirty mop water scented with bleach. The din was like the roar of the Friday night football game.

As Darci and I walked in, she pointed out a student in a mustard-yellow, three-piece polyester suit. "That's Chris Padgett. I'll introduce you; we attend the same church."

Hesitantly I agreed, and moments later I found myself meeting this atypical fellow. I don't remember much of the conversation, but it was apparent that Chris was very nervous. He fidgeted a lot and didn't have much to say.

After a short and clumsy exchange, Darci and I left and joined one of the long lines snaking toward the food. I avoided the breaded mystery meat and mushy noodles and headed for the hamburgers, fries and chocolate shakes. And I didn't give Chris Padgett much thought, at least not then.

It didn't take long for me to realize, though, that Chris was wild about me. I was blown away by his enthusiasm and flattered to see a guy so excited just to be in my presence. I had never dated someone who made me feel so precious.

OUT OF MY LEAGUE:
CHRIS MEETS LINDA

I first saw Linda Dodge at Bayshore High School. Man, was she hot! But seeing was all I could do. After all, what would she want with someone like me?

Linda was not just any girl; she was a varsity cheerleader and a karate expert, and most people acknowledged that she was amazingly beautiful. What I'm saying is that everything about her was perfect. She had perfect hair and perfect eyes. In fact, her eyes were sooo blue, strikingly blue. And her body was wowsome! Man, she was fine!

Not only that, Linda was in the popular group. She had brains, and I could barely spell branes. She was the cream of the crop.

Imagine seeing the best of something and realizing that you have no way to obtain it. She was untouchable, definitely out of my league. I didn't have a chance.

I remember our school talent show. Let the emphasis rest upon the word *show* and not *talent*, because most of the participants were less than gifted. Picture in your mind's eye, for example, a girl cloaked in neon spandex, frills and ballerina shoes, doing a dance to "The Flying Purple People Eater."

Linda, on the other hand, a picture of unfathomable Ninja abilities, was wearing a silver-sequined gee, the uniform people in martial arts wear while doing a roundhouse kick to someone's head. She performed a routine to a song from the *Rocky* soundtrack. As I watched her kicking and sliding around on the stage floor, I knew I was in love. All that came to mind was how nice it would be to get to know her in any and every way possible.

Of course, with all those karate skills, she could have kicked my butt if I made any wrong moves. So I sat in the audience, silent and drooling, wondering how I might actually meet this living lethal weapon.

I did think that with a perfect plan there might be hope that we could connect as a couple. My mind set to work on a brilliant sketch. I had to strategically wow and dazzle this dynamic girl! My creative wit had to amaze even myself.

I didn't really have many ideas about how to win this woman's heart. I only had the aching desire to be with her, which probably wouldn't be that convincing. In fact, I was willing to settle for a "hello" in the hallway or a quick glance from a distance because I was afraid that if we did meet, she would realize that this goofy guy before her, namely me, was more annoying than interesting. And then it would all be over, my hopes would deflate, and she would move off in someone else's arms.

Introducing myself to Linda was the first step. By the grace of God I ended up meeting her through our mutual friend Darci. Isn't this the way many of our plans unfold? Our friends turn out to be intermediaries for us.

This particular day Darci was walking with Linda to the school cafeteria. By the action, possibly, of Divine Providence, I arrived at school that day wearing an outfit selected for its intrinsic shock value. My poor mother was horrified by my choice of clothing every morning. On this day I sported a delightful mustard-yellow, polyester, old-

4

man suit, exceptionally out of place that year. I was pre-retro with no thought of any eventual in-demand fashion trend.

Linda had on her cheerleading uniform, which reminded me that I wasn't good enough for her. Pushing past this sober truth, I gazed with reckless abandon at her beckoning beauty. I was overtaken by her smile and the way her hair caressed her neck. And did I mention her body? Oh, yeah, I did.

Standing there, I knew I looked as dumb as I felt, and there was nothing I could do to make a good physical first impression. I distracted her from my odd appearance, from my legs twitching nervously, from my nose that resembles a launch pad from *Top Gun*, by taking a stab at small talk. The brilliant words flowed from my lips like water cascading from the river of knowledge.

"How is your egg doing?" I asked.

She laughed, and I was madly in love. She said that for a week she had to carry around an egg for her life-management skills class.

I smiled like the idiot I was, and I don't remember much of the conversation. I could barely comprehend that she was talking to me. I was enamored, entranced, para-lyzed by her presence. She and Darci went off to join the cafeteria line, leaving me to ponder my next move.

I began looking for Linda around school and any-where else I thought she might be. Some people call this stalking, but I prefer to view it as extreme interest in one of God's splendid creatures.

A few days later when I saw her driving home from school, I ran a red light just to keep up with her. The fine points of the law meant nothing to me, now that I was consumed with love. I lived off the few glimpses I caught of her at school and on the road, willing to run over anyone who got in my way.

Spotting the Right One

1. What do I look for in a guy?
    a. the perfect stud
    b. Richie Rich
    c. a potential life-mate
    d. nothing, as long as he asks me for a date
2. What do I look for in a girl?
    a. anyone who will go out with me
    b. anyone who will go out with me
    c. anyone who will go out ...
    d. a potential life-mate

DATING STANDARDS: WHAT ARE YOU LOOKING FOR?

Chris

I wanted to date someone I was physically attracted to, someone who was intelligent and funny. I wanted a girl-friend with Christian morals, but I also sought some physical contact. I wanted to kiss, touch and go into new and uncharted territory physically, even though I knew

6

that would conflict with my Christian upbringing. I have always been a rather sensitive person, and I never wanted to use a girl for personal pleasure, but I hoped there would be mutual interest in physical exploration.

I was very aware, though, that integrity and faithfulness should be cultivated in serious relationships. My mother and father divorced when I was five, and I could see the fallout from a relationship jostled off the right track because of a lack of integrity. Our broken home was difficult not only for my parents but also for my sister and me. I knew that I would not want to offer that instability to my future children when I married.

Even when I was in high school, looking for a companion was not just an experimental phase for me. I wanted to have fun, but I also wanted to find someone who would share my values, goals and dreams.

Many young people, like me, long for more than a just a fling. For these it can be extremely difficult to handle the knowledge that the person they are falling in love with has been sexually active in previous dating relationships. They may begin to worry, "What will this person expect of me? How will I measure up compared to this person's previous dates? Will I satisfy him or her compared to other physical encounters?"

When Linda and I began dating, I had heard that she had been promiscuous. But I didn't care. I figured that if we did hit it off, then it wouldn't matter what our bruised pasts looked like.

I was wrong. After we fell in love, I was constantly wondering if she had been happier with the other guys than she was with me. When we became sexually active, I fretted about not being the only one in her life who had shared such intimacy with her. It was difficult to see other guys she had dated and resist the urge to strangle them.

The more I fell in love with Linda, the angrier I became with her past. It killed me to know that the woman of my dreams had been involved in moments of varying intimacies. It actually was years before I realized that she was honestly and totally committed to me for the long haul. As mind-boggling as it seems, somehow she was in love with me as much as I was with her. Linda reassured and comforted me, giving me confidence in regard to our relationship. I would not have had to battle with those feelings, however, if I had been the only man in her life.

The ideal situation, obviously, is to remain pure. Why? For one thing, most of us are not looking for a mate who has been around the block more times than the ice-cream truck. As Christians we want a morally pure mate who won't cheat on us when we buckle down and offer commitment. In these relationships we are all looking for a moral *yes* that actually means something.

I think the picture of the Blessed Mother's entire *yes* to the Father is relevant here. She did not hold back any part of herself when the angel came to her. Our Lady freely embraced the will of the Father and let her *yes* encompass the fullness not only of the Incarnation but also of

Calvary's sacrifice. Mary's *yes* mattered for all of us.

What will the repercussions of your *yes* in dating mean? Will you say yes to purity or to self-gratification? Your choices will reverberate down the years.

For sure, some of you need to reassess what you're looking for when it comes to dating, just as Linda and I did. In other words, it's important to establish standards that reflect integrity, purity and maturity. These are the standards that should guide you as you consider a potential date.

Maybe the real question you need to ask is "Should I be looking for a date at all?" Certainly dating situations in secluded or otherwise tempting settings put you at risk for sexual experimentation. Group activities provide safeguards, but that doesn't mean you won't experience temptation. Growing in holiness and a firm commitment to chastity has to be part of your personal program if you plan to date and stay pure.

If you're anxious about finding a future spouse, trust that if God wants you to marry, he will lead you to that mate in his time. Relax. Keep your standards high.

We do a disservice to God and the one we are to be with when we burden the gift of a genuine relationship by promiscuity. As you grow older and your dating experiences multiply, so can your sexual experiences. If you are promiscuous, your actions eat away at your life and the lives of your partners. You begin to realize that what you were looking for in the beginning—fun and companion-ship—is not the same as what you look for in the end, a deep, permanent, committed relationship that will pro-vide the foundation for your family.

Here is the key thought: What you do in the beginning of your dating experience plays a part in who you become in the end.

Linda

I love Chris. He is a great husband and father, and I feel fortunate that this wonderful guy is my life-mate. Chris has changed and matured during the eighteen years we have known one another, but I could see the seeds of his terrific character during the early years of our relation-ship. He was different from the other guys, so our rela-tionship was also atypical.

Chris was the first boy I could talk to about God. We would spend hours on the phone discussing our thoughts about heaven. My family was not attending church regu-larly when Chris and I first met, but he invited us to his church and we all went. In fact, my mom went on to attend that place of worship for years, and my sister was married there.

I recall being warned by a friend that if I started dat-ing Chris, I would have to get my life right with God, because Chris was regarded as a religious guy. When I heard that caution, I felt relief and enthusiasm because I desperately craved a renewal in my spiritual life.

Even in the promiscuous years of our relationship, we never stopped attending church and talking about God. We even chose a Christian college over a state school. While it was good that we were concerned about our faith, the fact is that we were flagrantly ignoring Christian truth about sex outside of marriage. We knew it too.

Our entry into the Catholic church would come several years later, so we didn't have the benefit of the sacrament of reconciliation. But we had other guides to chastity that we conveniently put aside. Our relationship was far from the best that God desired for us.

Nevertheless, one of the main things that drew me to Chris was his spiritual life. Though it was not perfect, even our classmates noticed it. We agreed on the fundamental truths, unlike the basketball player I dated who believed in reincarnation or the other guys who never even mentioned God unless it was to take his name in vain.

Religious compatibility is an extremely significant factor when considering a dating relationship that might lead to marriage. If you have to drag your partner along in his faith, the situation will usually not improve after you have become comfortable with each other.

Another thing that drew me to Chris was that it was obvious that he truly liked me. He was so nervous on the phone that he needed an outline of what he wanted to say. I was completely flattered. The other guys I dated were self-confident, self-centered "idols" of the school. Chris was humble, genuine, even insecure. He knocked my socks off. I never felt that I had to pretend to be someone else. We were real with each other.

And you know, that hasn't changed. To this day I have never doubted Chris's love for me. He has always been open about how he feels and what he thinks. We still have great talks. We still enjoy being together. We miss one another when we're apart.

The bottom line in looking for a potential date is to consider whether this person would be someone you'd be interested in as a possible mate. Don't waste your efforts on people with whom you don't line up spiritually. "Do not be mismatched with unbelievers. For what partnership is there between righteousness and lawlessness? Or what fellowship is there between light and darkness?" (2 Corinthians 6:14). Set your standards high, and trust God to bring the right person around.

Bad Pick-Up Lines

10. I can't take my eyes off of you.

9. Which one of you is free to go out tonight?

8. Hey, what's your name again?

7. My mom makes my lunch too.

6. I think Britney is awesome; you look like her.

5. I have skills: nunchaku skills, bow-hunting skills...

4. I've been waiting for you all my life.

3. God told me I am supposed to marry you.

2. What's a pretty girl like you doing in a church like this?

1. If you were a booger, I'd pick you first.

THE WEIGHT OF THE MATTER: THE IMPORTANCE OF THE RIGHT LOOK

Chris

I have never been on the cover of *GQ* magazine. Actually, I have never been on the cover of any magazine. I am not an example of the "in shape" guy, and I inherited a big nose from my father.

I can't grow facial hair, at least not enough to make people acknowledge it as real facial hair. Most people think my upper lip is just a little dirty when I haven't shaved for a few weeks. I can honestly say that as a teenager I would shave in faith, hoping that the action of shaving would somehow stimulate my hair follicles. It didn't work.

Everyone says, "Oh, you're so lucky that you don't have to shave every day." These are people who look like Chewbacca from *Star Wars*.

Along with my big nose and lack of facial hair, I have another interesting feature: dark circles under my eyes. My sister has them at times, and I figure it is something of a family trait. I heard it has to do with poor circulation, and this could be true, since I have had a heart condition since birth. The partially closed valve in my heart was the main reason I wasn't allowed to participate in competitive sports during my school years.

So in some ways I am a physical oddity. This is not much of a concern for me. I truly like who I am. Honestly, I'd like to be a bit more in shape and at least confident that my circulation is fine, but all in all I am happy with my existence. I have learned to live with myself and am not too bitter.

I feel I have been loved and appreciated by others for my gifts and talents despite my physical limitations. All over the country, at conferences and retreats and workshops, people have listened to my hyperactive rambling, and some have even enjoyed it. My wife loves me unconditionally, and my kids receive me heartily. I am even funny enough sometimes to cause myself great comic relief.

What am I saying all of this for? I am God's child, and he has formed me hairless, big-nosed and with the occasional dark circles under the eyes, and it seems to be OK with him. In all of my uniqueness I have found his love to be constant.

This is a message for our times. Too often young girls compare themselves to magazine pictures of females who have been painted, chopped and altered into an unnatural state of perfection. Guys struggle to grasp what is currently cool and hip so as to feel confident as they walk the malls or cruise the strips.

Today's younger generation is bombarded with the lie that what is visible is all that matters. I see on television and in movies women and men who shop for body part replacements as if they are buying milk from the supermarket. And these are our "heroes"? The media, Hollywood and society shun those who don't conform to their shallow standards.

This message has led young women to starve themselves in order to achieve a physique appropriate only to young children. I know of a girl who hangs on by a thread because of the lies she believes. Her body is literally eating itself due to anorexia.

I see a generation of young people trying to get attention by any possible means. But let's face it: Youth are not the only ones who fall prey to this deception. Adults flock to spas, gyms and plastic surgeons in a desperate search for the coveted fountain of youth.

I am speaking as a leader of youth but also as a father of eight children. I hope and pray that my sons and daughters know that no matter where they go and whom they meet, their father and mother, who are captivated by them, have established their lives on a foundation of love and unconditional acceptance. I hope and pray that they don't believe the lies that permeate our society regarding physical and fashion standards.

So what if you have a big nose, need glasses or have only one arm? God, who makes something out of nothing, is in control. If the one who has been, is and will always be says it is "very good" (see Genesis 1:31), then it is, in fact, good.

Are you listening to the correct voice? The Word who brought light into the darkness, who opened the eyes of the blind, who freed the possessed and the oppressed, who made the lame walk, the deaf hear and the dead rise is proclaiming out loud that your existence is enough! Do we have ears to hear this Word amid the many voices of our generation?

These voices that hiss our supposed weaknesses, declare our unfitness and come slithering in a variety of forms to compete for our lives are real, not imagined. They come at us loud and clear through television, radio, magazines, books, peer pressure and even parents.

We can counter these many voices only by listening to the one Voice that matters. Listen to God say, "I love you." Even when I see myself as physically inadequate, and even when I know I am limited in my abilities, God's voice reassures me of my completion in him. I stand as a testimony to our Creator God.

We come back to the point and place of balance. We remind each other that we are loved and accepted by the Father. All of us need this reminder.

Be content with yourself and how God made you. Take pride in the unique design that God gave you. In the Holy Scriptures we are reminded that outward beauty is vain (see Proverbs 31:30). It is by the heart that we will be judged.

Conversation Starters

1. I can't wait until leap year. It will be my fourth birthday.
2. What do you think about the situation in Iraq?
3. What is your favorite TV show? movie? music?
4. I heard that it was a great Super Bowl. Did you watch any of the play-offs?
5. Do you like to read? I just finished a book by Dr. Seuss.
6. Do you like sports? What is your favorite team?
7. My sister says I talk too much; do you think so?
8. Have you ever had braces?
9. Did you ever play Ms. Pac-Man at an arcade?
10. When you burp, how far can you get in reciting the alphabet?

Question: *Are there really differences between men and women? If so, what do they mean for me as I get to know members of the opposite sex?*

Linda

I am a person who doesn't care much for words. To be told "I love you" matters less to me than being shown that love. Furthermore, I'm not easily offended by words, and I rarely believe what someone says until I see it happen.

The opposite is true for Chris. He is very optimistic and easily believes someone. He can be greatly wounded by someone's comments, and he seeks affirmation with words. As a result of our differences in communication, we have to work hard at dealing with each other in his or her "language."

Of course we're not always successful. My shrewd tongue and insensitive heart have bruised Chris's spirit too many times. Yet when I simply say, "I love you, Chris," I meet his need for our love to be confirmed. As for my needs, when Chris changes a dirty diaper without being asked, he communicates love and affection loud and clear.

These are personal differences and not necessarily gender-based. Our experiences don't even line up with other couples' experiences. It is true, though, that there are differences between men and women even though there is a wide range of variation in those differences. In general, women tend to be nurturing, and they relate in a personal way to people and situations.

Women in the childbearing years also have to adjust to the hormonal fluctuations that accompany their cycles. Some women experience moodiness and sensitivity at various points in their cycle; some women don't. Many women would benefit, though, by developing an understanding of how their cycles affect them so that they can learn to control emotions that might affect their relationships.

Young women in the first few years of puberty can have an especially hard time sorting through monthly hormonal changes. As they mature—and if they pay attention—they usually find it becomes easier to manage any emotional flare-ups that might accompany their cycle.

Men, on the other hand, tend to be abstract and impersonal and focused on their work. Properly handled, their greater physical strength and drive to produce work-related results can create a safe harbor for a family or for others in their sphere of influence.

On the negative side, men can be inclined to dominate women, to dismiss and overlook them. In the extreme they can express their "will to power" through verbal and physical intimidation. Young men, as they cope with the hormonal surges that accompany puberty, need strong guidance so that they learn to control their emotions and desires and grow into mature and responsible men.

The two sexes also deal differently with a physical relationship. In general, a young man's core attraction to a sexual experience is the physical enjoyment. A young woman, on the other hand, is usually drawn at first to the emotional satisfaction of a sexual relationship.

I'm sure curiosity plays a large part in a girl's decision to become sexually active, but in the beginning her experience will tend to be less physically fulfilling. What appeals to her most is the feeling of being loved and desired. Unfortunately, in immature and casual relationships, it is that emotional vulnerability that opens her up to great suffering.

The differences in men and women are complicated to understand and frustrating to deal with. If you feel as if you're utterly bewildered as you try to figure out the opposite sex, relax, you're part of a significant majority. If you consider these basic differences and mix in unique personality styles and background experiences, you can see how difficult it can be for men and women to establish solid relationships and communicate effectively with one another. That is why unconditional devotion is necessary for success.

Padgett's Ponderings

There is an old nursery rhyme, "Rub a dub, dub, three men in a tub." I don't feel comfortable with this. Does anyone else consider this a bit too edgy to be sharing with our children? What is a dub?

Another odd rhyme: "Jack be nimble, Jack be quick, Jack jump over the candlestick."

This rhyme doesn't make sense. How does jumping over a candlestick measure "nimbility"? Why did Jack need to be quick? If the candlestick is small, doesn't this encourage young people to have small goals? We can only hope that it was a candlestick of great proportions.

Will we ever know? Who wrote these tales anyway?

Question: *Is there something wrong with me if I don't want to date?*

Chris

Actually, there is nothing wrong with you if you don't want

to date. All the superficial games couples play with one another can be exhausting. To be honest, I'm not so sure dating is all that it is cracked up to be.

This is especially true today, when many in the dating realm are looking primarily for a sexual fling. Too many people think that a sexual experience is the goal of a date, and the initial flowers and candy, the dinner or movie, is the bait. No Christian should have anything to do with this sort of dating scene.

The ideal scenario would be for guys and girls to simply relax and be who they are as they journey closer to the Lord. As we've said before, dates that take place in a group or with another couple or two who share your values are the best approach, especially for young people who are still some years away from marriage. And as far as marriage goes, if God is as big as we've heard he is, then surely he can help bring that special person to you at just the right time.

So maybe you have discerned that you are not interested in dating or being with someone other than your family or friends right now. That's fine. If you can be content with who you are, how God made you and where you are now, then when or if you do meet someone special, you will be sure to have your head on pretty straight regarding who you are as an individual.

People often identify themselves according to the status of the one they are dating. Others try to satisfy their internal loneliness by entering a relationship with someone who gives them undivided attention for the first time in their life. We can see why there are many problems in these relationships, because no one is ever able to be another person's final fulfillment or answer to loneliness.

There are tons of reasons why people don't want to date. Some people are simply afraid, which isn't such a bad thing! Some have other interests or volunteer work they want to pursue. Some people don't date because they feel called to a life of celibacy, either in religious life or as a single person in the world. This is a lifestyle that Jesus lived, and frankly, he didn't seem to lack humanity or masculinity because he didn't date.

If you don't want to date, then don't. If you feel pressured to date, I suggest you wait, because pressure is not a reflection of the freedom we have in Christ. Don't put yourself down if you feel uncomfortable with dating. It could be that God is sparing you a whole heap of problems that others will have to address as they continue on their relational roads. Be sensitive to God's voice within you in this matter.

Linda

There's only one thing wrong with you: you don't recognize that your decision not to date is completely sensible! Most serious dating relationships should be left to those considering marriage. There is so much in your life right now that is more important than dating.

It is never too early to invest in your spiritual life. The history of the church is filled with stories of young people who gave themselves to God and, as a result, changed their corner of the world. Venerable Maria Teresa Quinta, a twentieth-century Spanish Carmelite, said, "Jesus has good taste, you know, and he wants youth with all its joys and its dreams."[1] She wanted to give God the first fruits of her young life, not ask him to settle for second best.

Committing yourself to going deeper with Christ does not imply that you are signing up for a religious vocation, although there is great grace and honor in that. Those who choose to enter the vocation of marriage also need a strong religious foundation on which to build happy, healthy families. Becoming involved in church and community service will not only give you great peace and joy; it will also prepare you to be generous and other-centered in a relationship later on.

Your education is also essential. More often than not, your education will play an important role in your plans for the future. Do your goals require a college degree? If so, the earlier you begin to prepare, the more likely you are to gain admission to the college of your choice and to qualify for scholarships.

Your family is another aspect of your life worth your time and attention. Put some effort into getting to know and understand your parents and siblings, those God gave you first. I tell my children that if they can't get along with family, how will they ever be able to develop successful relationships with others?

Modern concepts of dating are generally burdensome and certainly not innocent. The world's casual attitude toward love is not healthy, nor is it what God intended. Society says that falling in and out of love is normal and acceptable. Modern culture places little importance on commitment. The casualties of this social system are the hearts and minds and emotions of young people. Guard your heart, and do not allow it to be victimized by the fickle behavior of contemporary society.

How to Prepare for a Date

For Guys

Get dressed; look sharp.

Brush your teeth.

Brush them again.

Put deodorant on, and some cologne just to be sure.

Bring your wallet. Put some money in it too.

Clean your car out before you pick her up, *not* during the date.

Get directions or make sure that she does (we know how guys are with directions).

Meet the parents with a smile (your teeth should be clean).

Open the car door for her; when closing it, don't slam it on her legs.

Treat her like a queen.

For Girls

Get dressed, fully dressed.

Put on a sweater, even if you live in Florida.

Don't brush your teeth; this will keep him at a distance.

Don't put on deodorant; see above explanation.

Bring a cell phone or fifty cents in case you need to call home.

Prepare your family to meet your date.

Greet him with a smile but not too friendly of one.

Stand at the car door until he opens it for you. If he doesn't, go back inside your house.

Only bring enough money for a phone call home. That way he'll have to pay for everything.

Try not to burp in public.

Blame the toot noise on the seat.

THE STORY CONTINUES:
"CHEZ PADGETT"

Linda

We have affectionately titled our first bona fide date "Chez Padgett" in an effort to make it sound more impressive and elaborate than it really was. Prior to this first rendezvous Chris called now and then, and we chatted about simple matters in order to get to know each other better. Finally we arranged a time to go out.

I asked him what I should wear so that I could get a sense of what type of date it would be. He said to dress nicely but casually, so I chose my light blue sweater and cream pants.

Now, my dad was not a very large man, but he ruled the house with his voice. During World War II he was a Marine. At the age of eighteen he guarded prisoners who were in for life. In a way he wanted to protect his three daughters with the same intensity. There were specific rules that were not to be broken:

1. No one calls after 10 P.M.
2. No one comes over uninvited.
3. Always come home by your curfew.

Last but not least, a guy would have to meet Gilbert, my dad, if he wanted to take out one of his daughters.

On the evening of the big date I waited in the kitchen for Chris, due to arrive any minute to be put through the drill. To my surprise, an ex-boyfriend showed up at the door without an invitation and apparently under the influence of drugs. He and his friends sat on the couch amusing my dad with a guitar. I was dumbfounded. To top it all off, my dad didn't seem to mind.

I was embarrassed when Chris arrived, and it was obvious that the situation disturbed him. It had to have been uncomfortable to be introduced while an ex-boyfriend sat in the living room sharing a good time with my father. We quickly excused ourselves and drove away in Chris's gray Chevy station wagon.

I was a little confused when we pulled up in front of his house. At first I thought he had forgotten something. My puzzlement mounted when he opened my car door and led me to a screened porch on the side of the house.

Awaiting us there was a room aglow with candles, a table set for two and classical music in the background. Ever the gentleman, Chris pulled out my chair. As Chris took his seat, Jason, his best friend, entered the room wearing a tuxedo, with a towel draped over his arm as if he were a waiter in an expensive restaurant. He greeted me with a kiss on the hand and welcomed us to "Chez Padgett."

The meal was surprisingly delicious, especially considering the fact that Jason and Chris had made it. The main course was hamburger Parmesan, accompanied by sparkling grape juice. A dessert of ice cream and mint cookies followed. I had never experienced such a perfect dinner.

At one point I looked up and saw three faces peering at us through the window. Chris's mom and sister and Jason were getting their evening's entertainment by watching us. His family was checking us out!

After dinner we retired to the family room and watched a movie. Chris chose a classic, *Blazing Saddles.* I can't remember much about the movie, but I do recall Chris' lifting his shirt and showing me how he could suck in his stomach to make himself look as if he hadn't eaten for months. He also gave me his senior picture with a special note on the back.

As the evening came to an end, we headed back to my house and parked in the front. Next came that moment of awkwardness that inevitably followed my first dates. Should I just go in? Will he try to kiss me? Should I let him?

To my surprise, Chris actually asked my permission for a kiss. My face turned red with embarrassment. I approved, and he leaned over and gently gave me a nice simple kiss, nothing intense or messy.

I went into the house and told my mom about the evening. Sitting on the couch in front of the Christmas tree, I knew that the evening was special and that this fascinating guy was truly unique.

Chris

I will forever remember our date entitled "Chez Padgett." This was not your normal restaurant. My best friend Jason and I had decorated the screen porch for the romantic evening, putting soft classical music on to blanket the background with a warm and inviting atmosphere. Jason dressed up in a makeshift tux to act as our waiter, and he attended to last-minute details while I readied myself for the date.

I encountered an extremely awkward moment when I went to pick Linda up. Her father required that I meet him, but this was only a slight concern as I entered the house. There, sitting next to her dad, was one of Linda's ex-boyfriends with a couple of other guys from our school.

I, nervous as could be, worried that this guy from her past was somehow still in the picture. Was I the victim of some cruel joke? Apparently not. They were all stoned and had come by uninvited to get some food and act like jerks. Their arrival was not only a surprise to me but also the whole Dodge household, especially my embarrassed date, who had retreated upstairs, out of the way.

Despite the initial setback, we headed out the door with a sense of relief and expectation. She looked like a song, elegant and melodic, gliding into all of my senses with such grace. I was overwhelmed by her smile, enveloped in her presence. She was too good to be true.

We arrived at my house, and Jason was quick to welcome his guests. That little kiss on her hand as he greeted Linda was not part of the pre-production plan. Who did he think he was, putting his nasty lips on my girl's hand?

Jason served the dinner with simple elegance, and Linda was all smiles. In the middle of the meal I looked behind me, only to notice my sister, mother and Jason peeking through my bedroom window, which overlooked the porch. They were not so subtly spying, and I thought it made the situation funny and kind of romantic. Somehow I knew we were making history.

The evening was waning as we entered the living room to watch *Blazing Saddles*, a classic movie meant to push all of Linda's romantic buttons. This was probably not the best cinematic choice, but I had a weird sense of humor.

I drove her home, and the little car sputtered and spurted in front of her house as I asked if I could give her a goodnight kiss. My heart was thumping out of my chest. What if she said no? I would feel like such an imbecile.

My fears were for naught. She nodded her willingness, and I leaned over and gave her a small kiss.

I was blown away! Floating home, it all seemed like a dream. I couldn't quit thinking about her. My luck had somehow changed. I was out of my league—but still in the game.

MEET THE PARENTS? AUGH!

Linda

Even though this seems like a terrifying thought, if you are still living at home, it is a good idea for your parents to meet the person you are going out with. This was a strict rule in my home when I was growing up. My parents were older than most of my friends' parents and held more traditional ideas. Looking back, I'm grateful for their conservative viewpoints.

Every boy who even expressed an interest in going out with me had to pass the "meeting with Gilbert" test. My dad could easily intimidate a young fellow, and I lost many dates due to his reputation. In fact, when Chris first said he wanted to date me, a friend warned him of the impending meeting.

There were several boys I desperately wanted to date in high school, but my parents would not let me. Somehow I was blind to the fact that these guys were nothing but trouble, in most cases mixed up in drugs. At the time I was incredibly frustrated, yet deep down I knew my mom and dad were right.

God has given you parents to lead you in life when you're young and to be a source of wisdom and strength even after you're on your own. Sometimes these parents fail to do the job as well as intended; nevertheless, they are the immediate authority in your life, at least while you are still dependent on them. Your parents have lived longer and experienced more than you and can often spot a questionable character quickly.

Furthermore, since meeting someone's parents is a difficult thing to do, the process can weed out prospective dates who are not sincere. The guys who only wanted a good time (whatever that would have been) didn't invest any effort in getting to know my dad. In some cases they never even showed up. The fact that Chris was willing to put up with the Gilbert Drill showed me that he was serious about pursuing a relationship.

Chris

Yes, you should meet the parents of the girl or guy with whom you're going out. Why? If you're serious about getting to know your date, then his or her parents are anxious to get to know you. It's also important to see the guiding forces behind the one you find so attractive. It does matter.

So what if they don't really understand what you're all about? Maybe you won't be the best of friends, but it is imperative that you at least extend the courtesy of a general introduction.

Sometimes there are insecurities associated with introducing one's parents. But no matter how rough, tough and terrible your mom and dad are to your date, he or she should still meet them. If you have found true love, it will endure regardless of how hard-nosed your parents may be.

As for me, I struggled with Linda's father. Countless times I fought the urge to deck him for the verbal abuse he heaped on his own family. I was repulsed by the way he spoke to them, and our own conversations were not much better as the volume increased with each passing moment. We couldn't agree on much of anything.

But it was important to me that I engage in some civil dialogue with Gilbert, since I wanted to be with his daughter. He was the gatekeeper, and even though it was hard to keep the lines of communication open, my love for Linda enabled me to do whatever it took to continue being with her. I really did want to honor Mr. Dodge and not be disrespectful.

Should I have met him and worked at our relationship? Absolutely and so should you if you are serious about the person you want to date. Having the blessing of the parents can smooth the way for many opportunities and make it easier to get permission for date nights.

Will you ask your wife to disassociate herself from her parents once you are married? Not if you're smart. You will want to meet them and accept them for who they are. They might not be the best reflection of your true love, but they were part of her formative years. And once you marry their child, you will be interacting with them for some time.

Another point to consider is that you may be the conduit of God's grace to a family in need of a genuine encounter with Christ. You could lead them back into communion with the church. Your actions can have eternal consequences, allowing Christ to shine through you to your date and to his or her parents.

Mr. Dodge passed away a few years ago. As I stood by his bed in a hospital room in Florida, I looked on this man with whom I had struggled for so many years. Even after Linda and I married, I had many uncomfortable discussions with him. As much as possible Linda and I had tried to love him.

Mr. Dodge and I eventually came to grips with one another. After all, he was now grandfather to my children. The final years of his life brought about a taming in his wild spirit. In his last few months we went to visit him as much as we could.

In our last lucid conversation with him before his dementia fully set in, we spoke of eternal things. As Linda and I drove away that evening, there was not one feeling of ill will toward this man. All we longed for was his peace with Christ.

I bring this up because Gilbert was part of the package: when I got Linda, I also got her family, specifically her dad. This particular portion of the deal was not easy to handle, but in the end love made a difference.

Ideally your date's parents will be interested in getting to know you too. I suggest praying for them on a regular basis. Who knows, one day you may be calling them mom and dad!

What Not to Say to Your Parents When They Meet Your Special Someone

From the Girl's Perspective

I *think* he believes in God.

He says school is not really that important.

His parents are out of town for the weekend.

I think all of the charges have been dropped.

He wants to be a musician when he grows up.

From the Guy's Perspective

She can burp the alphabet.

When she goes to school, I guess she does pretty well.

I don't know if she's a Christian. She says God's name a lot though.

I got her number off the bathroom wall.

Her favorite food is lettuce.

Question: *Help! I need some cheap and creative date ideas.*

Linda

Some of the most memorable dates Chris and I had were the ones that didn't cost much. The next outing after "Chez Padgett" provides one of those cheap date memories.

We went to the beach with a candle, a blanket and some packed food. It was still light, and the beach was semi-full. It was December, and even in Florida the weather was freezing. The wind cut through us like a knife and blew the blanket and sand all over.

We escaped to the lifeguard house for protection from the wind, but we couldn't tolerate it there either. Chris and I didn't want to give up too easily, so we went to a restaurant, ordered an inexpensive meal and asked the waitress if we could set our candle on the table. She agreed, and we dined in style.

Looking back through the years, I see that Chris and I had an interesting and adventurous dating life. We both grew up in families where money was hard to come by, and we were used to being financially challenged. We didn't require a lot of money to have a good time. The important point wasn't what we were doing but that we were together.

In the college years, when holding down a job was nearly impossible, money was practically nonexistent. Yet I think we had some of our finest dates during that time.

My roommate Teresa and her boyfriend Tony joined us in many of our adventures. Not only did these double dates provide accountability, but they also added two more personalities to the date, making the time even more enjoyable and exciting.

Our excursions usually started with the guys picking us up. They rarely had a plan but would make one up as the night went on. Once, for example, they picked up Teresa and me and then drove us around town with no apparent sense of purpose. They would stop at random moments and get out of the car to confer about what we should do next.

The highlight of the evening came when they went into a grocery store and returned hiding something in their hands. They told us to close our eyes and open our mouths. Trustingly we did as requested, and in went a PEZ candy. We wrapped up the evening by sharing the treats in the cartoon dispensers. What a silly date, but I still remember it fondly.

Another date ended with the four of us hanging out on top of a parking garage overlooking a very classy retail community in Palm Beach, Florida. That night the great expense was for bottles of bubbles. We blew these bubbles over the edge of the roof, and they drifted past unsuspecting couples out for a romantic walk.

Dating can help you get to know someone who could possibly be the one with whom you will spend the rest of your life. Therefore, don't get hung up on trying to impress your date. Set up experiences that draw you together, lead to a deeper understanding of one another and are innocent and simple. If your date has the correct motives in being with you, he or she won't get upset at the lack of elegant dining and expensive gifts.

Chris

My suggestions can help you keep your date night pure as well as within the confines of a tight budget.

Get a couple of your friends together and collaborate on a dating event. For example, combine your bucks, buy some bait and stand on a local pier casting your lines out for the big catch. Then build a fire where you can all sit, talk and cook the ones that didn't get away. Going out with a group has a double advantage: you save money by splitting the cost, and you have people to whom you are accountable for your behavior.

How about gathering a group of friends at one of your homes for a cool game night? Pit the guys against the girls, or play couples' Trivial Pursuit.

If there are places to hike, get some friends together for a day trip. Combine funds and go bowling. Visit museums together; most offer discounts for students.

Regarding dates for the two of you, parks are public places, and you can have some real fun and meaningful talks together. Go to the library and investigate colleges you might want to attend together or careers that might interest you. If you like music, go to concerts together; if you enjoy theater, investigate the plays being performed in your area.

You can also do things for people less fortunate than you. Go to a soup kitchen together and serve dinner for the needy. Visit the lonely in a nursing home or hospital. Not only are you investing in other people's lives, but you also are laying a foundation of service that will have a positive impact on you individually and on your relationship.

When Linda and I were dating, I was extremely poor but pretty creative. We loved to walk on the beach and have picnics. One time I did a little photo shoot of her at different sites around town. It was fun, and we have some of the pictures as memories.

Write stories and read them to each other. Write songs and sing them to one another.

Learn how to have fun together without the pressures of sexual temptation. How do you do that?

First, don't place yourself in a situation that will allow you to fulfill your desires. As we've said before, don't be alone if you can help it. If you want to have a romantic dinner, invite another couple, drive to the restaurant together but split up once you get there. This way you will have some privacy but won't be tempted to get into the car and cruise to a quiet parking lot in the mall, only to be caught by the security guard doing things you shouldn't be doing.

Choose your movies carefully. Hollywood has a way of fitting sexual content into the most wholesome stories.

In general, be careful and don't pretend you are above temptation. Often the simple dates can be safer yet more adventurous than extravagantly expensive ones. You don't have to be rich and famous to have fun and make a great impression.

Cheap, Creative and Corny Date Ideas

Play board games or cards at your house.

Go to a park and amuse yourself on the swings and slides.

Go to an open field with friends and play ball.

Go to a restaurant for dessert or chips and salsa.

Watch the sunset together.

Buy some chalk and play hopscotch or foursquare.

Take younger siblings to the zoo with you.

KISS

K Keep in mind that you might be kissing someone else's future spouse. It's not pleasant to think of your potential husband or wife making out with another person.

I Intimacy is exciting, but it brings with it an avalanche of responsibility and reality that can only be handled in the confines of marriage.

S Save your best kiss for the "I do."

S Stop. Kissing outside of marriage does not include the tongue. Don't look at kissing as a form of entertainment.

What Do You Think?

Write your answers to the following questions in your personal journal.

1. Are you aiming for the best when investing your time in a relationship?
2. What kind of experience of dating did your parents have? Ask them.
3. What character traits in a person are important to you?
4. If you are dating someone now, why did you decide to pursue this relationship? What do your parents think of this person?

Thoughts to Consider

How do we evaluate a person's character? How do we get past image and reputation to catch a glimpse of who a person really is?...We need to carefully observe three areas—how the individual relates to God, the way he or she treats others, and the way this person disciplines his or her personal life. (Joshua Harris, *I Kissed Dating Goodbye*)[2]

I have chosen to follow God's standard, and I've communicated this to my teammates....I have respect for myself and the women I've dated. I try not to focus on idle thoughts that can turn to temptations....I know there's something better for me if I wait. (NBA all-star A.C. Green)[3]

Honor your father and your mother, so that your days may be long in the land that the Lord your God is giving you. (Exodus 20:12)

Section Two

The Fall

Chris

As Christmas vacation ended and we returned to high school, nothing was the same in either of our lives. Linda and I were a couple, and boy, did we love it! All was fresh and explosive. Life focused on us.

We did everything together when our schedules permitted and found creative ways to cope when they didn't. We had to be in constant communication. Writing notes, talking on the phone or just thinking about one another—that was daily life. Love notes passed to one another between classes (for all seven periods) enabled me to get through the day. I don't know if we managed to actually learn anything at school during this time.

At home, when we were apart and unable to talk on the phone, we made audio recordings for each other. We'd fill a tape with sixty minutes of our myopic understandings of love and then give the other the tape. We don't recommend this: it can cause extreme embarrassment when someone—not your parents, you hope, or years later your own children—finds these tapes.

Our behavior was obsessive and led us to do things we never imagined. Linda left a job at which she excelled just so we could work together at the local grocery store. The store's uniform was a lime green polyester number so

Linda went from looking great in her short skirts to resembling the character we affectionately know as Gumby. She was still strikingly attractive!

We skipped school regularly until school officials caught us. I was suspended for a few days, and Linda was refused a scholarship opportunity due to these poor choices.

Our love continued to grow, until we made a choice one evening that changed our relationship irrevocably. We didn't intend things to pan out in this fashion, but once begun, everything tilted into a new dimension.

That evening we had sex for the first time, in my car. We excused ourselves by saying that in our hearts we wanted to completely give ourselves to each other. This seemed the logical next step in such a serious relationship.

Growing up, both of us had learned that premarital sex was wrong, but in our passion we quickly justified our sin. As a result, doors opened in our spiritual lives that allowed the enemy to get a foothold. We felt trapped in a vicious cycle, unable to gain control. We couldn't figure out how to stop.

We felt terrible about our immoral behavior but experienced defeat after defeat as we struggled with the desires of the flesh. There was no way that I wanted to stop. When you stumble repeatedly in the same sin, you begin to feel hopeless that you will ever achieve lasting victory over it. That sums up our situation. As much as we tried to avoid sexual promiscuity, our flesh managed to find every opportunity to satisfy our desires. It was war within and without.

I was terrified that my mother would somehow find out how corrupt her child had become. She would be crushed if she knew I was sexually active.

One day as I came into the house, I heard my mother say, "Chris, explain to me what's on your bed." I knew she was baiting me for the kill. This was not an expression of interest but a tactic she employed when confronting some issue with me. Whenever I was in trouble, this redheaded wonder called Mother would place the convicting evidence on my bed, wait to hear my pathetic excuse and then dish out my deserved punishment in a supersized format.

I stumbled into my room, my heart beating frantically. My life was in peril, but I didn't know the specifics yet. And there on my bed was an unused condom out of its wrapper. Fear surged through me as I turned to face my mother. Panic held me in its grip as I tried to think of anything that would explain such incriminating evidence.

I mumbled some less-than-enlightened comment like, "Well, since it's here on my bed, that means we didn't use it." It was something as stupidly nonbrilliant as that. I knew at that moment that my mother was disappointed in me. I realized that God was disappointed too, and truthfully, Linda and I were disappointed with ourselves as well. But we seemed powerless to break the hold of sex on our lives.

Some people think that physical sexual expression is a natural reaction to raging hormones that overwhelm all young people. Certainly the hormones are animated, but just as certainly we could have controlled them, especially if we had never started having sex to begin with. Rather than quench our desire, the physical expression just made us want more.

Our consciences reminded us of our sin, but we found ways to numb them. I was no longer thinking clearly, having pretty much given my entire self over to being with and experiencing Linda. All the values I once held dear as a child were moved to the back burner of my heart. Life centered on my giving myself to the one I loved.

Deception seemed a small price to pay in order for us to be together. We sacrificed the trust of our parents on the altar of selfishness.

During these turbulent times we cried many tears of repentance and made commitments we didn't keep. We felt we had no power to help us stop what we had begun. We needed a miracle. We needed a transformation!

SHAME

Linda

Have you ever felt that God has turned his back on you in shame? That he is so ashamed at what you are doing that he can't stand to watch? That's exactly how I felt every time Chris and I participated in premarital sex. Despite our sincere aspirations in the beginning to have a spiritual relationship, we fell into the same trap into which many have fallen.

For both of us this relationship was not the first that involved sex. The difference in this relationship, though, was that both Chris and I knew better. We both grew up knowing that sex was to be saved until marriage, even though no one ever explained the importance of this moral standard. So we surrendered to the feelings and accepted our sinful behavior as normal.

A large part of me enjoyed the promiscuity, and why not? Sex was intended to be fun. But the other part of me knew I was playing with fire. I knew the sex I was engaging in was not the best sex God intended for me to experience. How could it be? I was using it as it was never meant to be used.

When I look back on that period, I remember the many great times we had that didn't involve sex. We made the mistake, however, of assuming sex was an appropriate means of building our relationship. Our weakened spiritual life could not counter the strength of sexual sin. This sin held us and would not let go. We justified our actions by saying we wanted to marry each other someday.

We also found solace in the idea that sexual experimentation was supposedly normal for teens. Looking around our high school, it seemed that everyone was sexually active. I assumed that the hurt and emotions that accompany promiscuity were natural and normal feelings that teenagers experience.

This was incorrect, of course. There were plenty of students who were stronger than I and able to say no to temptation. As a result they didn't have to live with the fears of hurt, pregnancy and sexually transmitted diseases as well as the dread of our parents' finding out.

Our refusal to control our physical obsession led us to do things we would never have considered before. Once Chris lied to his mother and told her he was spending the night at a friend's. As soon as the TV distracted my father, I snuck Chris in through the back door to spend the night with me. We were terrified of getting caught and so got very little sleep. Chris left early the next morning feeling that the whole event was a bit too risky.

Stupidly, we repeated this affair at Chris's house. I lied to my parents about where I'd be that night and crawled through Chris's bedroom window. The next morning I hid under his bed while his mother demanded to know the reason for the locked bedroom door. As his family prepared for church, I escaped undetected, passing his blind grandmother on my way out the front door.

What were we thinking? Our lives had become a breeding ground for lies and deception. Sin propagates sin.

Not only that, but our tunnel vision made us neglect everything else. School suffered, family suffered, faith suffered and eventually our relationship suffered. Our bond began to unravel as a result of our promiscuity; rather than strengthen our relationship, sexual involvement nearly destroyed it. We fought constantly. Deception, which had become the norm in our dealings with others, infiltrated our own relationship. Things spun out of control. Everything needed to change, or we were not going to make it as a couple.

Even though we eventually gained victory over this stronghold, the effects of our sin would linger for a long time. As a result of our sexual intimacy, I developed a premature emotional dependency on Chris. This caused great confusion in my heart when I started to grow spiritually. I wanted all that God wanted for me, but I was so tied to Chris that if I had had to choose between the two, I would have been inclined to disregard God. I was consumed by fear that God would take Chris away.

I was controlled by these feelings because I had already united myself with Chris in a way that is suitable only for married people who are forging a permanent life together. If we had waited until marriage to express the sexual side of our love, I wouldn't have had to deal with the emotional confusion that affected me for years.

Question: *What if I never have sex?*

Chris

I used to fly to visit my dad and grandparents as a young person. It occurred to me on a number of occasions that if the plane were to crash, my one wish would be to quickly have sex with someone while in flight so that I didn't have to die a virgin.

I longed to know what physical intimacy would feel like. I'd imagined it enough. The idea of dying before having had sex was something I wasn't prepared to accept. What a catastrophe that would be! What an incomplete life! Even the possibility of being with Jesus for all eternity didn't compensate for the thought that I would arrive at the pearly gates without experiencing that bit of earthly bliss.

Worse, Scripture says that in heaven couples won't be given in marriage. In other words, no sex! It was now or never. Every flight attendant became the object of my eye.

Fortunately, I never had to face this situation in my youth. Interestingly, I can barely endure the slightest turbulence when flying. I would have been hurling in an emergency, ruining any hope of achieving physical intimacy while the plane plummeted toward the earth.

God asks us to trust in his complete knowledge and love when it comes to sexual matters. If you don't have sex before you die, then I am sure that God, who is bigger than you've ever thought or imagined, has reserved the best for you, beyond the joys of physical intimacy. He is able to make something out of nothing; surely he knows if you should have sex before you die.

The question is, will you trust him? Do you acknowledge that he is worthy of your complete and total trust?

You regularly trust fallible humans. You trust that your teachers know what they should teach you, for example, and that your vehicle has been constructed properly.

So too, within relationships you have the opportunity to depend totally on God for something as precious as your sexual future.

Jesus was a virgin. Mary was a virgin. Countless saints, priests, nuns and regular folks like you have not had sexual intercourse, and they are no less men or women because of abstinence. In fact, many have given their sexuality to the Lord as a gift. No doubt the reward they receive in eternity will surpass the momentary pleasures they have given up in time.

We all give ourselves to someone. The question is, to whom are you giving yourself? Is it to Christ, in complete trust that he will guard your gift of virginity as you await his leading for your life's vocation?

Sex does not equal love. Sex before marriage delivers guilt, heartache and disappointment. Sex just to know what it feels like is a complete distortion of what that gift between a man and a woman is all about.

When I was in college, I heard a speaker recall a conversation he once had with his daughter. She was frustrated and felt awkward because she was a virgin and all of her peers seemed to be sexually active. She felt a bit out of the loop. Her dad looked at her and said, "In one moment you can be like everyone else in your school, but they can never be like you again." That is so powerful!

As a virgin you have a special opportunity to give to your future mate a part of you that is personally unique. The sacrament of marriage reflects the intimacy that

Christ has with his bride, the church, and his total, permanent commitment to her. Sex is meant for marriage because marriage is a permanent commitment that embodies and is a sign of God's permanent, "for-better-or-for-worse" love for each of us. God doesn't love us and leave us.

Distorting this gift not only blurs your understanding of the sacrament, but it also clouds your understanding of what real love is. If you have reserved the gift of your virginity for your future spouse but die before giving it, you have not been robbed of anything. Rather you have testified with your life to the true meaning of love.

Linda

When I was a teen I had this exact fear. The church my family and I attended placed a lot of emphasis on the end times and the return of Christ. In 1986 an evangelist came and said that Jesus was going to return by the end of the year. I was just starting a relationship with my first boyfriend, and fear overtook me. Although I wanted to see my boyfriend saved, I didn't want to go to heaven a virgin.

Unfortunately, I chose to deal with the second issue. I never witnessed to my boyfriend, but we did become sexually active. Needless to say, Jesus didn't return that year.

You never know what the future holds, so don't worry about your virginity. If you die a virgin, nothing is lost and heaven is gained. But if you get married having already given your virginity away, you will not only feel regret on your wedding night, you will also have to deal with issues in your marriage that the chaste never have to confront.

I once heard a man say, "Just because I haven't had sex yet doesn't mean I won't be good at it when I do." The sweetness of the fruit will be better if you are patient and wait until God's time.

Question: *How far is too far?*

Chris

This is probably the question young people ask us the most, and I can remember wanting to know the answer to this when I was young. The question reveals a lot about a person and where he or she is spiritually. In other words, the moment our experience with the opposite sex becomes a matter of how much we can get away with before problems arise, that's the moment we must reevaluate our approach to relationships.

How far is too far? For some it may be spending too much time with the other person. For all, anything beyond holding hands and a light kiss good night is probably going to get you in trouble. Heavy kissing, including French kissing, stroking, close embraces—all these are highly stimulating and designed to lead to one conclusion, sexual intercourse. Oral sex is real sex and is never acceptable in a chaste lifestyle.

One sign that you have gone too far is that you begin pushing the barriers of what you wouldn't allow in a previous date. Here is a basic rule: if it's covered, you ought not be messing with it! And if it's not covered and should be—low-riding jeans and bare midriffs leave plenty of exposed skin—the same holds true.

I have four daughters, and one day they will want to date. I will say, "You are not yet thirty, so the answer is no." If a young man comes to our house, Linda will demonstrate a few of her karate kicks. This will cause him to seriously consider the things I say to him about the date he is about to go on.

I don't want my kids coming to me later in life saying, "Dad, how far is too far?" I want them to comprehend the special gift they have within themselves. Both Linda and I strive to instruct our sons and daughters to know who and what is worthy of their time and attention. We want to teach them how to discern a man or woman of integrity from one enveloped in self. We pray that the truths we share concerning chastity will sink in.

Lord willing, our children will not place themselves in positions of compromise. In the end it is going to be their individual responsibility to apply moral truth in real-life situations, just as it is your responsibility.

Here's a basic guideline: establish clear boundaries that you as an individual will not compromise. If you are a teenager, follow your parents' lead regarding how late you can go out. If you are in college or on your own, keep reasonable hours; things can get strange as the night moves toward the morning. Respect the direction you receive from those you consider mentors in your life.

How far is too far? So the kissing doesn't bring lustful thoughts? What planet are you living on? Is your date an alien?

Most of us who remember kissing, and specifically French kissing, can honestly say that the thoughts and feelings that accompany it are more dynamic than a simple "How are you doing?" peck on the cheek. Be prepared! Too far is when you realize you are not leading with your head but rather your, well, let's just say "bubbly warm, fuzzy feelings."

How far is too far? The moment when passion replaces morality, imagination ignores honesty, and actions destroy standards.

Things to Consider About the Other When Getting Serious

· has a relationship with God vs. only uses God's name in vain
· takes relationships seriously vs. is in and out of relationships
· your parents like the person vs. your parents look for their face on *America's Most Wanted*
· values chastity and purity vs. gets impatient with your "goodness"
· has goals for the future vs. wants to party a little more before thinking about the future
· likes the way you are vs. compares you to others
· has friends who build him or her up vs. has friends who carry his or her mug shot in their pockets

More Cheap, Creative and Corny Date Ideas

Go on a picnic.

Go to the mall and dream of all the things you can't afford.

Go to a thrift store, buy outrageous outfits and put them on for a public appearance.

Go to a church or youth group concert.

Make sandwiches and take them to the down-and-out in your area.

Question: *Won't sexual intimacy improve our relationship?*

Linda

As I said earlier, premarital sex nearly destroyed our relationship, although in the beginning the intimacy seemed blissful. Here's what happened: sex began to take over, and it eventually became all we wanted to do. As a result, essential aspects of the relationship suffered.

Sex became a game. Where can we do it that we haven't tried yet? How far can we push the limit before we get caught? Our behavior got more and more careless. Once the security guards at the mall caught us.

All along the battle in our consciences raged. I was more affected at times than Chris, and so we would argue and the divisions would deepen.

When we finally broke the iron grip of sexual sin, Chris and I were able to develop a true friendship without the confusion of sexual involvement. Our intimacy grew in other areas. We enjoyed just being together. We focused on developing our spiritual life. We spent long hours in conversation about God, the past and our future.

As a result today, so many years later, we have a strong level of communication. Chris is my confidant and companion. There is complete trust and vulnerability between us. We have told each other our deepest and scariest thoughts without fear of rejection.

But sex didn't get us to this level; friendship did. This closeness didn't develop during our promiscuous sexual life but in the years of chastity that followed. Had we continued down the road of premarital sex, we would have been too absorbed in or confused by our sexual activity to build a lasting relationship. I don't know what would have happened ultimately, but it wasn't looking good.

Promiscuity not only had a negative impact on our ability to form a solid friendship, but it also had a negative impact on the early years of our marriage. By participating in sex before marriage, we developed selfish habits. We were concerned with our own needs and wants and not very concerned about what God wanted for us as a couple.

Even though we knew God had forgiven us and we had changed, the choices that we made when we were dating resurfaced as a source of tension in our marriage. I continued to struggle with memories and leftover guilt feelings from premarital experiences. As a result, it took time for me to accept the gift of God's undefiled marriage bed.

The bottom line is that it would have been much easier on our long-term relationship if we hadn't participated in premarital sex.

Chris

No, sexual intimacy won't improve the relationship. Emotional and physical realities become bigger and harder to process after sexual intimacy.

When I was growing up, my father made it clear that if I treated a woman with respect by considering her sexual happiness and not merely my own, then I should not be ashamed about practicing safe sex. After high school graduation Linda and I went to Scotland to visit my father, who was administering an overseas program for college students. Linda and I shared the same room for the five weeks we spent there. My dad knew we were sexually active and allowed it as long as we were "safe." Our behavior wasn't a moral problem in his eyes; he thought Linda and I were old enough to make our own choices. My dad's acceptance and encouragement, however, didn't change my internal realization that what we were doing was wrong in the eyes of God.

I never told my mother about that European experience. She would have killed me! Actually, her disappointment would have destroyed me. My mom taught my sister and me to live a moral life in accord with Scripture. She made it clear that biblical standards were meant for real-life situations; they weren't just some unattainable ideal in a book.

That meant no sex before marriage.

Like me, many of you come from broken homes. Maybe, like me, you also have one parent saying that sex with your date is cool as long as you practice safe sex, while the other parent insists that you apply biblical standards to your behavior.

Many times I embraced the freedom my father's approval gave me. Nevertheless, I couldn't silence the warning voice of God within when I crossed the lines in physical intimacy. I am proof that this persistent call to holiness can be ignored. Yet even when I numbed myself to the truth, my spirit was never fully at peace. This in-between state wasn't a pleasant place.

The sexual intimacy between Linda and me seemed fun and mature in the beginning because of its obvious gratification. But I can honestly say that the two years we were sexually pure before marriage were the most gratifying years of our dating relationship. Why? Because we began to experience and know each other in the proper relational context.

These two years of waiting, self-discipline and willingness to sacrifice our sexual desires taught us the real meaning of love. Love wasn't pretending to be what we were not—a married couple. It wasn't freedom to fulfill our desires whenever the urge hit. Real love was the two years of building trust in each other and in God's plan for us. It was mutually sacrificing physical desires in order to avoid quenching the desire for God that was blazing in our hearts too. Real love was more than I had imagined it to be and infinitely more rewarding.

When our union was finally blessed in marriage, the physical intimacy we shared was better than I had ever experienced. Within the sacrament of marriage we were free to express ourselves intimately without fear or feelings of guilt.

Question: *Why do I feel bad every time I have premarital sex?*

Linda

We are blessed with the gift of the Holy Spirit, who convicts our consciences of wrongdoing. In fact, having guilty feelings is a good sign. It means that you have not gone so far astray that you have become deaf to the voice of God.

Our Creator is not a killjoy. He knows how much fun sex can be; he came up with the idea in the first place. He asks only that we observe the boundaries he has established because he knows how damaging sexual involvement can be outside those boundaries.

All you have to do is look around at American society to see the effects of the so-called sexual revolution. Pregnancy outside of marriage is commonplace. About a million babies are murdered every year through abortion. Sexually transmitted diseases are widespread. Pornography, infidelity, rape, incest and molestation give further evidence of what happens when humanity steps outside the boundaries God has established for sex.

His still, small voice whispers his will into our hearts.

If we have the courage to tune out the voices that urge us to satisfy all our desires, we just might find the interior peace in which we can hear him speak.

Chris

Every time I had premarital sex, I struggled with guilt. Even when I had wandered from God's love and was a wretched backslider, I still couldn't shake the feeling of wrongdoing when I gave in to this sin. God puts this moral check inside us so that we can stop and ask ourselves, "Do I truly want to go down this road? It is against what I believe and know to be virtuous, so am I going to willingly move forward with this sin anyway?"

I recall trying to sin without feeling guilty but never succeeding. I asked myself, how could having sex with Linda be wrong? After all, I loved Linda and was going to marry her. Why couldn't I just do what felt so right?

Many argue that the guilt that accompanies sin is merely the result of brainwashing by an oppressive church with its decayed religious system. But this feeling of guilt is actually from a God who cares enough to put safeguards within us so that we can obey him and avoid spiritual calamity.

In high school I was pretty good friends with a girl who was funny and enjoyable to be with. We dated a bit, and one night we had the opportunity for a sexual experience. In my passion I wanted to continue heading down the road we were on. We actually discussed stopping if we thought guilt would dominate after the experience.

I insisted guilt wouldn't be a problem, rationalizing it in my mind (yeah, right). It was OK, I assured her. I kid you not, right after we were done I felt so crappy that it blanketed everything!

This girl was willing to give herself to me emotionally, physically and mentally, but all I was considering was my immediate gratification. I liked her, but I knew I wasn't in love. I was ready to have fun but not ready to handle the intensity of what we were entering into.

Within the month I ended the relationship and broke her heart. It was hard on her and hard on me. I know that if I had chosen purity that night, we would have avoided tremendous pain. I knew at the time I persuaded her to have sex with me that she was more emotionally involved in the relationship than I was. This just added insult to injury.

It is hard enough to break up with someone, let alone someone you have bonded with through sexual intimacy. My regret for that relationship lingers today. Our sins don't affect just us but others as well.

Conviction and guilt were the warning signs God provided to keep me from making that mistake. I ignored them. He promises to always give a way out of temptation, but deliverance doesn't usually come as thunder and lightning from heaven. Most of the time God speaks in a respectful whisper, reminding us of what we already know.

He expects us, for example, to use common sense. He asks us to take to heart the teaching of the church and the guidance of our parents. And he expects us not to just think about the truth but to *act* on it.

Even though he expects obedience from his children, in his love God never forces his will on us. He wants our obedience to come from love and a desire to please him. He made us his children, not his robots.

When temptation comes your way, remember that those feelings of doubt and conviction are his voice urging you to be careful. Do yourself a favor: listen to these warning signals and not the urgings of your gut. Regret is another intense feeling, and you don't want to live with it forever.

Question: *Why* don't *I feel bad when I have premarital sex?*

Chris and Linda

Not all of you reading this book feel guilty about having premarital sex. Through television, music, literature, the Internet, self-appointed cultural leaders and in many other ways, our society has become desensitized regarding matters of morality. Popular TV shows such as *Friends*, with its six attractive young stars constantly referring to their sexual exploits, have an insidious effect. They wear us down with their humor and health (no one ever complains about having an STD on sitcoms like this). The net effect is that sin looks attractive.

The idea of restraint or delayed gratification seems unnatural in today's culture, and avoiding intimate expression for any reason other than personal is considered oppressive. Christians and other people of faith who promote sexual purity are regarded as hopelessly out of touch.

If you're going along with today's cultural norms, sooner or later you'll find your resistance to sexual temptation worn down. It will become easy to ignore your conscience. If you numb yourself long enough, if you ignore the truth that God has revealed about who he is and who we are in relation to him, if you continue to feed yourself the lies our society offers, you will certainly lose that healthy feeling of guilt that warns you to avoid certain behaviors.

Our generation is made for better things than this. We are capable of resuscitating our consciences and standing in opposition to society's trends.

OFF TO COLLEGE

Chris

As high school came to a close, we had to decide which college to attend. Linda was toying with the idea of going to the University of Florida in Gainesville. A few schools had offered me scholarship money for music studies, but nothing was set in stone.

One day I received a phone call from Palm Beach Atlantic College, a small Christian school on the east coast of Florida. The admissions recruiter suggested that Linda and I attend a day of orientation to see if we might be interested. For some crazy reason we agreed to go.

Linda and I had never traveled that far together, so we prepared for our journey with great excitement. We were not familiar with the eastern coast of Florida and expected the trip across the state to take about seven hours. We stuffed a cooler with all the essentials: Swiss cake rolls, candy and soda. Since we had to be there first thing in the morning, we headed out in a Toyota Tercel at about 11 P.M.

To this day I am shocked that our parents allowed us to make that all-night trip. Didn't they realize that it wouldn't take seven hours to get there?

We arrived in West Palm Beach at about 3 A.M. The trip only took four hours—what were we thinking? Totally exhausted, we reclined the car seats and slept in a parking lot at the college until 6 A.M. Then, with a few hours to kill before the orientation began, we decided to drive over the bridge to Palm Beach and gawk at the various mansions peppering the exclusive area.

Palm Beach, Florida, is a unique environment completely unlike our hometown. As we sat at the open drawbridge waiting for a yacht to pass, expensive vehicles rarely seen in Bradenton, Florida, surrounded us. A Mercedes puttered in front, a Jaguar sat on our left, and a Rolls Royce gallantly brought up the rear. As we drove onto the exclusive island, it was like a scene from a movie. Glam and extravagant displays of wealth were everywhere, dazzling our eighteen-year-old eyes.

We returned to the college for several hours of orientation and a tour of the campus. We liked what we saw. As we sauntered back to the car, however, we realized that we had locked the keys inside. Exhaustion and frustration hit hard, but at that point a student went out of his way to assist us. He befriended us, asked questions and ultimately helped us get the doors open. He made a lasting impression on me that reflected on the school itself.

There was something right about Palm Beach Atlantic College. It seemed as though we would fit in there. I wanted to be a part of a student body that could express God's love in the practical way that the helpful student did for us. Linda and I both applied and were accepted.

Palm Beach Atlantic turned out to be the perfect college for us. There our lives would be transformed, and our relationship would mature.

Things Not to Say to Your Date

- Have you gained weight?
- Did you get that outfit at Goodwill?
- What was your name again?
- Is your sister dating anyone?
- You're not ordering dessert, are you?
- Is your hair really that color?
- Would you like a mint?
- It doesn't look like you work out.
- Can we get separate checks?
- My friends say I'm stupid to date you.

What Do You Think?

Write your answers to the following questions in your personal journal.

1. Evaluate yourself honestly. Have you crossed the moral line in a dating relationship?

2. If you have, do you feel guilty or not? Do you rationalize your behavior?

3. Realize that the choices you make individually will affect you collectively. What responsibility do you have for your dating partner's spiritual welfare?

4. Read the story of the Prodigal Son in Luke 15:11–32. If you have fallen, are you ready to return home? How do you think the Father will receive you?

THOUGHTS TO CONSIDER

Shun fornication! Every sin that a person commits is outside the body; but the fornicator sins against the body itself. (1 Corinthians 6:18)

Think about it. If you and your boyfriend are not faithful to God's laws, what evidence is there that you will be faithful to each other? (Matt Pinto, *Did Adam & Eve Have Belly Buttons?*)[1]

When two people can't find anything to say, they're tempted to fill in the silence by getting physical. While making out does cover the embarrassment and even leaves a feeling of

becoming closer, it never substitutes for communication. If you try to make it a substitute, you will
wreck your relationship. (Tim Stafford, *Worth the
Wait*)[2]

I began to notice that the more I had [sex], the
more I wanted. I had always heard the excuse that
having sex was the way to get rid of sexual tension,
but the opposite was true. Having sex increased
the desire. (Josh McDowell and Dick Day, quoting
a teen in *Why Wait?*)[3]

When people in love go to bed, there's self-sur-
render involved. They're naked and totally
exposed before each other. The act of love is not
just a uniting of bodies, but it is also a uniting of
minds and spirits. There is a spiritual exchange
even in the most casual, one night stand. You
can't really have sex casually. It's not a casual
thing. Your spirit is involved. (Tim Stafford,
Worth the Wait)[4]

Statistics show that the length of time that relationships last between unmarried men and
women who live together is usually less than two
years. (Thomas and Donna Finn, *Intimate Bedfellows: Love, Sex, and the Catholic Church*)[5]

Section Three

The Change

From Promiscuity to Purity

Linda

After only eight months together, we left for college. Palm Beach Atlantic had a firm curfew and strict rules. I finally saw my opportunity to develop a spiritual life.

At home the friends I hung out with and my basic lifestyle made it difficult to live out my faith. I had attended school with the same group of kids for thirteen years and felt trapped by their expectations, pressured to conform to an image that they would approve. The campus milieu was different. It fostered my spiritual life by providing fewer distractions and by accepting and promoting Christian truth. I felt free to recreate my image.

My first roommate, however, was similar to the high school friends I had left behind. If I had not been firm in my decision to change, I might have continued on my old destructive path. But I saw this time of independence as a new beginning. I wanted more in my relationship with God. I started reading the Bible and making time to pray.

As a result of this new fervor, the crack in my relationship with Chris opened into a chasm. He was moving in a different direction than I. His musical choices went from bad to worse, as he began to favor violent and even

Satanist bands. I couldn't stand being in the car with him when he turned on his music.

We often ended up in heated arguments. It seemed that he was doing things just to irritate me. He chewed tobacco, for example, even though it made him sick, and he began lying to me. There were moments when I would look at him and think, "What has he become? Why am I staying with him?" Familiarity was part of the reason we stayed together because at first we had no other friends at this new school.

But also, despite the difficulty in our relationship, I did love Chris and in a way needed him. Consequently we continued to struggle with sexual sin, although I became increasingly conflicted about it. I craved purity, yet I was not strong enough on my own to overcome what felt like an addiction.

The situation reminded me of the candy binges of my childhood. On Halloween night I would eat sweets until I felt sick. The next morning, if offered more sugar I would refuse. My body craved something nutritious.

That was how my spirit felt during those beginning months of college. I was tired of being spiritually sick and wounded. My spirit desired life, and I knew that life only came from Christ. I needed to pursue him and find him. And I really wanted Chris to take this journey with me.

Our relationship remained in the same rut until Thanksgiving break. A few days prior to this short vacation, I had intense pain in my jaw, the result of a cyst that had formed on the root of a tooth. The cyst was a rare side effect from an operation I had had in eighth grade for a broken jaw. I went home, and the day after Thanksgiving I had minor surgery to correct the problem.

Late that night I was recovering in bed when the phone rang. The person on the other end asked me what I was doing. Assuming it was Chris, I was annoyed. Earlier that day he had helped my mother bring me home. He should have known that I was doing nothing but trying to recover.

I quickly realized that the caller was not Chris but probably an ex-boyfriend. I tried to make light conversation, but when he became obnoxious I hung up and called Chris. I told him about the rude call, and when I said I suspected it was my ex-boyfriend, Chris exploded in a fit of rage. He decided to go to this guy's house and confront him. First, though, he thought he should call the offender to warn him that death was pending.

When Chris called he discovered that this was not the guy who had called me. But more than that, he found out that this former boyfriend had become a Christian. Chris ended up going to the guy's house to hear the full story of his conversion. We spent the remainder of the weekend hanging out with his group of friends, all of whom had surrendered their lives to God.

A month later, over Christmas break, Chris went with this group of new Christians to a Bible study. He came away a changed man. I recall sitting in his car and hearing him relate the experience. We could see right away that our relationship needed a transformation. We discussed steps to bring our life together in line with God's will. I rejoiced over this new commitment to walk together with God.

During the second semester of college, we were both on the same page spiritually and relationally. Even though we did not overcome the sexual stronghold overnight, the situation began to improve. The turning point came when we totally surrendered each other and ourselves to the Lord. All of a sudden God was our primary focus rather than one another. We gathered a circle of friends who shared the same commitment to live for God.

We also devised regulations for ourselves that would help us remain pure. Some of these rules were pretty radical, but we were serious about change. Minor adjustments wouldn't do the trick when temptation threatened to overpower us.

Since I loved Chris and wanted to help him grow in holiness, the first issue we tackled was my wardrobe. Chris told me honestly what clothing caused temptation. I adapted my wardrobe accordingly. I had to give up wearing shorts, at least when I was around him.

Chris stopped listening to violent and occult music, and we stopped going to movies, since so many were filled with sexual images or references. We were poor college students, so it helped that movies were simply too expensive.

At some point along the way our relationship became chaste. The fruit of that chastity was a dear friendship and camaraderie that had been lost when we were having sex. We learned to love each other without selfish intentions.

The victory was that we remained 100 percent pure for the two years we continued to date before we married. On our long-awaited wedding night, I pictured God looking down on us, no longer ashamed of our actions. This time, sacramentally committed, we were enjoying his gift as he intended.

From Oppression to Freedom

Chris

Palm Beach Atlantic College grew from the Baptist tradition, a congenial choice for us since Linda and I were not Catholic yet. We were glad to be going to a school that had a religious foundation, even if our lives didn't reflect a thriving spirituality. In fact, I hesitated to call myself a Christian because of the moral choices I had been making. I wasn't interested in being a hypocrite, so I couldn't confidently speak of my faith to others. Linda and I both knew that the problem was a paralyzed spiritual life brought about by sexual promiscuity.

Deep in our hearts the longing to follow Christ remained. We wanted our words and deeds to proclaim this, though that rarely happened during these unsettled times. If we were going to mature as a couple, somehow our faith had to rejuvenate and dominate our lives again.

We had chosen a Christian college knowing that there would be no co-ed dormitories. We even had a curfew and got demerits if we broke it. We adjusted to this new way of life, but we still found ways to sin.

We didn't have the gift of the sacraments, especially the sacrament of reconciliation, but we repented in our hearts as best we could. What little spiritual life we had was unequal to the challenge; giving in to temptation seemed to be part of our makeup.

Those first few months in college I was falling apart. I was absorbed in extremely aggressive music. I had also been cutting myself with a knife, partially because I found it fascinating and partially out of the loneliness and internal unhappiness I felt. I was also reading about magic and occult situations and events.

Linda and I continued to struggle in our relationship. She was growing in her faith and wanted to be chaste, while I was falling further and further from my Christian roots.

The change in my spirit started with a class project. I was taking a basic required course on oral communications. I figured it would be effortless for me, an easy A. I had been involved in theater and music for most of my school years and was accustomed to speaking before crowds.

One of the assignments was to give a persuasive speech to the class for an allotted amount of time. I decided to speak about how to be a good Christian. I could recall better times in my spiritual journey and remembered being faithful to healthy Christian practices. I knew that regular prayer, Bible study and evangelization were important in a relationship with Christ, so I made these the key points of my speech. I felt like a hypocrite, though, given my own spiritual condition.

I began the speech but, unusually for me, felt a bit fearful and uncomfortable. Suddenly I felt light-headed and panicky, and everything seemed weird. I couldn't breathe properly.

The class could see I was falling apart before them. They cleared some chairs and helped me lie down on them as I struggled to pull myself together. I heard someone starting to pray. I don't remember all he prayed, but there came a point when he said, "Satan, the Lord Jesus Christ rebukes you!"

It was something like that and I promise, at that very moment, I felt a heaviness leave my chest. It felt as if a weight was lifted from my body. Not that I was possessed, like the girl in *The Exorcist*, but I was certainly oppressed and depressed. This prayer came as relief to my aching soul.

That event shook me up. I was keenly aware that my life had to change. Before I went around instructing others on how to know the Lord, I needed to do a bit of housecleaning.

On our first Thanksgiving break from college, Linda and I headed back home. There, unbeknownst to me, God was about to begin the transformation in my spiritual life.

One night I was under the impression that an ex-boyfriend had prank-called Linda. I was determined to address the situation in a way that would let this kid know he was barking up the wrong tree. When I discovered that he hadn't made the call, he went on to share with me how his life had changed since he found Jesus. Face to face with my nemesis, I could see that he was not lying.

My head was spinning. I felt even more guilt when I realized that I should have been the one witnessing to this kid, and not the other way around. I had been brought up in the church, and he had not. My mother taught me Bible verses, and I went to vacation Bible school, participated in church plays, attended revivals. I was more than aware that Jesus instructed us to forgive our neighbors and love our enemies, but I had somehow become my worst enemy and greatest obstacle.

For the next few days I kept running into other students I knew from high school who were now following Christ. A few weeks later, during Christmas vacation, I was hanging around with some of these guys discussing music. One of them said that he had an electric guitar he no longer used. I could have it, but I'd need to pick it up back at his dorm at a university in northern Florida.

I had an extreme interest in heavy rock music and needed an electric guitar to play some of my own, so I didn't hesitate to agree to go get the guitar. I knew that he and his friends would invite me to attend the Bible study that had touched their lives so dramatically. I figured it would be great to go and be touched by God, but I feared that I had strayed too far from his reach. I was a mockery to the faith. I was used goods. I was without much hope at all.

Sure enough, the guys invited me to the Bible study at a house down the road. Reluctantly, my nerves on edge, I went with them. Entering the home, I was struck by the love the mother of the house extended to me and to those already there.

I met the guest speaker, and he asked me about my faith in Christ. When had I given my life to Jesus? I ignored the temptation to mask my true feelings, and in all honesty I asked, "Which time?"

When did I give my life to Christ? The number of times I had vowed myself to his service were innumerable. Over and over again I had ascended to great spiritual heights, only to plummet to spiritual catastrophe. My "walk with God" had been more like a ride on a roller coaster, and at that point I was almost off the tracks.

The students gathered round and began to pray for me. There, in that living room, I met God in a way I had never experienced before. It was familiar yet new. It built upon earlier "conversion" moments, but it was defining for me, having felt so far from him for so long. I was changed.

It's hard to express, but I suspected that this was a special opportunity to start over. I snatched it, knowing that there was no guarantee it would be offered again. God had touched my life, and by his grace I didn't want to fail him. He had reached out and embraced me, and I was never going to be the same.

I went back to school a new man. The transformation started in my heart. It wasn't forced, and it wasn't the result of guilt. Instead I found myself falling more and more in love with Christ. I truly wanted to change, not just by renouncing blatant sexual sin but also by striving for discipline in prayer, knowledge of the Bible and more Christian fellowship in my daily life. I wanted to surround myself with people who were passionate about the Lord. These changes played a huge role not only in what I did but also in how I thought.

Linda was elated. She no longer had to be the spiritual leader; rather, together we could make a difference and fight to live what we so deeply believed.

As Linda and I transitioned from sexual obsession into Christ's gracious freedom, the sorrow for our failures was definitely extreme. I found, however, that for the first time in a long time I had the hope that Christ's love for me wasn't contingent upon my ability to be perfect in my dating relationship. Because of his love and his help as I met the challenge to rethink old thought patterns, each day held opportunities and victories.

Slowly we made our way out of the sexual trap. God's triumph manifested itself in our dating relationship as we maintained sexual purity for over two years prior to our wedding.

Please Pass the Dressing: A True or False Quiz

• There is no way to be in style and still dress modestly.

• The way I dress affects my date.

• Spandex is all the rage.

(Answers: You tell me.)

Question: *Does the way I dress really matter?*

Chris

Often questions about modesty have obvious answers. If you dress like a floozy, chances are you'll attract a loser; if you dress in a way that is seductive, chances are you'll be hit on.

Fashion is a huge part of how people express and perceive themselves. The jocks wear their style of clothes, and the preps dress in their particular way. People hope to reflect on the outside what they are trying to understand on the inside. This purpose-driven dressing is played out in dating too. Many want to look sexy in order to reel in the object of their desire. They want to make a statement: "open for business," "out to lunch," "petting zoo."

It should come as no surprise that the way a woman dresses can make a big difference in how a guy responds. Guys are visually stimulated. If you really want to attract a guy who is honorable and uncompromising, try a modest approach in fashion. Wear a bra, for crying out loud! You think I am kidding, but this undergarment is not considered superfluous by your male observers.

I know some girls who feel the need to dress seductively because they want to keep their guys interested. If a girl wears a mini-skirt, guys will scheme ways to sneak a peek. The truth is, the more they see, the more they'll want to see. How much are you going to show them before they want to sample the goods? Do you really want to be labeled as the loose and easy one of your crowd? Of course not, but labels are applied to certain packages based on the way they are presented and marketed.

A lot more can be said about modest dressing, but I think you get the point.

Linda

What's your motive for the way you dress? We women have to be honest and admit that we like the attention we receive when we dress a certain way. Chances are that as a young person you have a figure that will never be repeated again in your lifetime. It is understandable to want to flaunt it, but there are consequences to your clothing choices.

When Chris and I were struggling with sexual sin, the way I dressed advertised the obvious. The tighter and shorter the garments, the more the flames of lust were fed. When we reached the point where we wanted to be chaste, the dress code for our dates had to change.

As I mentioned earlier, for us the first thing that went was shorts. Chris wanted to be totally protected from potential lust, and my wearing shorts was a big problem for him. You might consider that extreme, but our desire to walk honorably before God was also extreme. We were desperate for change.

Luckily for me, the fashion at the time featured loose-fitting jumper dresses. They didn't reveal every curve, and they hung nearly to my ankles. We called them "holiness dresses." Today the styles are more seductive, but you can still be fashionable and remain modest. And don't worry, you can have a great but modest look without filling your closet with holiness dresses.

Keep in mind what the Bible says: "Resolve instead never to put a stumbling block or hindrance in the way of another" (Romans 14:13). You don't want to be held accountable for leading another person to sin by the way you dress.

Blessed Jacinta, one of the children to whom Mary appeared at Fatima, mentioned this concern nearly a hundred years ago: "The sins that bring most souls to Hell are the sins of the flesh.... Certain fashions are going to be introduced which will offend Our Lord very much. Those who serve God should not follow these fashions."[1]

Even as a grown woman I struggle with this issue. The Lord often reminds me that I need to be careful not to cause another to sin with his eyes.

I keep two thoughts in mind when shopping for clothes. The first is to be proud of my femininity and dress in a manner to accent that. The second is to honor the Blessed Mother and dress in a way that pleases her.

This doesn't mean that I always wear dresses but that I choose all my clothes—pants, sweaters, shirts, skirts—with dignity and honor in mind.

And let me throw you guys some advice: women might not be as visually stimulated as you are, but super-tight jeans and T-shirts carry a clear sexual message. Avoid these. And when you go out, dress in a manner that tells your date that she matters. Demonstrate respect by showing up in clean, neat and appropriate clothing.

Question: *What if I've messed up? What should I do now? Is it too late for me?*

Chris

We are living testimonies to the fact that even if you've messed up, God will forgive your sins and restore your life. Will you pay for your past? Are there consequences?

In many ways, yes, you will reap what you've sown. You'll remember things you regret doing, and you'll feel loss as you contemplate things you should have done. Desire is not going to magically disappear either, especially if you have been feeding it through your actions. That would be an incredible bonus, but most of us have to actively choose to change.

God's forgiveness, though, is greater than our sinfulness. His love is bigger than our selfishness. His power is greater than our weaknesses. His holiness is deeper than our impurity, and his acceptance is constant, despite our rejections. "God did not send the Son into the world to condemn the world, but in order that the world might be saved through him" (John 3:17). Although our actions call for rejection, God offers the repentant sinner forgiveness, healing and mercy as well as intimacy with him.

Our common bond as humans is that we have *all* messed up. Obviously, sin isn't the same from person to person, but we have all made poor choices. We have all wounded others and ourselves by things we have said or done or not done. The journey, though, is not over until it is over, and if you are breathing then it isn't over. God will rescue and revolutionize you. If you are a couple interested in starting over, he will enable and strengthen you in this commitment.

It is not too late, it is never too late, to take a step toward home. Remember the Prodigal Son in Luke 15? Like him, you might have wandered off and spent everything you had on wild living and then realized that your choices have left you devastated. You have reached rock bottom. Do you give up? No, you remember your Father's house.

As you take one step toward home, and then another, you see in the distance the Father running to you. He has seen you while you were still a long way off and comes to enfold you in his arms and celebrate your return. Does he despise you? No, he acknowledges you as his child. He demonstrates forgiveness by what he says and does, by his genuine warmth and acceptance. Will you receive it?

At home in his forgiveness, as his child, not his servant, he invites you to know and accept his love for you. He is bigger than your sins, circumstances and situations. Not only will he rescue you from your past, but he will also open a path to a new future. Choose the Father!

If you are acknowledging that you have sinned, then you are in a terrific position. Confession is the first step toward healing.

When Chris and I were in the grip of promiscuous sex, we weren't Catholics and so didn't have the benefit of the sacrament of reconciliation. This sacrament is a source of grace and strength. Also, the accountability that comes with confessing to another person is irreplaceable. I am less likely to commit a sin if I know that I will have to confess it to a priest.

God is always eager to forgive those who are genuinely seeking him and just as eager to help them stay pure. "For the grace of God has appeared, bringing salvation to all, training us to renounce impiety and worldly passions, and in the present age to live lives that are self-controlled, upright, and godly" (Titus 2:11).

The key to victory over sexual sin is changing the focus of your attention. How do you do that?

We Catholics have great tools to aid us in loving Jesus more. The first resource is the Mass. Attend Mass as often as possible because there is no greater prayer to transform and conform us to the likeness of Christ than this sacrament of sacraments. We can never be closer to the Creator than during those moments when Christ is literally within us. Cherish that time, and ask him for help to remain pure.

If you are unable to attend weekday Mass, practice spiritual communions. This is the custom of asking the Lord to come into your heart spiritually when you aren't able to receive him physically. The great Saint John Vianney, the Curé of Ars, said that when we feel our love of God grow cold, we should offer a spiritual communion. You can do this throughout the day.

Our affection for Jesus will grow as we practice desir ing him. And focusing our attention on him will keep the empty promises of immorality in perspective, while at the same time keeping us in the light and beauty of divine love.

To gain victory over sexual sin, it is also important to avoid falling into old traps. Consider what factors led you down the path of sexual immorality. Is the music you listen to suggestive? What movies do you watch? What magazines do you read? Are you using pornography on the Internet? Eliminate things that offer sexual stimulation or are cues for you to lower your standards of behavior.

Consider too that your sexual involvement may be a result of insecurity. Are you looking for love in all the wrong places? Do you believe that recognition from the opposite sex replaces the lack of attention you receive at home? Is popularity something you seek at any cost?

God will meet those emotional insufficiencies and give you solace. It is a good idea, too, to talk with a trusted adult for guidance and support and to see if professional counseling might help you resolve some of these personal issues.

If both you and your partner want chastity, then with the grace of God you can proceed as Chris and I did. If only you want it, then you will probably need to end the relationship. This could be the most difficult thing you've ever done, yet God will give you the courage you need. And if that person is meant to be your life-mate, God will restore the relationship when the time is right.

God's plans are always superior to ours. "The human mind plans the way, but the LORD directs the steps" (Proverbs 16:9).

More Cheap, Creative and Corny Date Ideas

Go to a cheap restaurant and study; at least you will be together.

Bake cookies together.

Go ice-skating, sledding, roller-blading, biking or hiking.

Go to the driving range or play miniature golf.

Make each other dinner.

After an Italian meal, burp the alphabet together. Maybe not.

Padgett's Ponderings

I have never been a big eater in the morning.

Some people wake up ready for eggs, bacon and cereal. As a child I saw my grandmother eating bran cereal, shredded wheat and other health-oriented products. I subconsciously felt it would be wrong to eat cereal that looked as if it had already been digested. Bran cereal is just plain wrong when all is said and done.

I recall TV ads for a cereal with *fiber* in its name. Every person in the commercial suffered from memory loss. This really discourages one from buying it. We have enough problems without consuming a breakfast cereal proven (commercials don't lie) to feed the tragedy of memory loss. What I realized about that cereal is that people didn't want to be reminded that they were eating something that is, in most people's minds, essentially a laxative.

Question: *What if a relationship doesn't work out?*

Chris

Don't freak. I look back on all of the date and relationship experiences I had, and I'm grateful that things didn't work out the way I wanted them to.

It is never fun to break up with someone though. Even when you want to get out of a relationship that is unhealthy, the conversation isn't usually carefree; feelings are bruised. Breaking up is especially difficult if you felt the person was, in fact, *the* special someone.

Christians should keep in mind the good news that God really is in control. It doesn't always feel that way, but he is and it makes a difference. If he is big enough to create the universe from nothing, turn water into wine, heal the sick and raise the dead, then he is able to understand and help you in your times of trouble. He understands the bigger picture and is not taken off guard.

If while you were dating you said or did things that you need to apologize for, or if you should have done something but didn't, then you may need to hash out these issues during the break-up. But if the relationship just didn't seem to click, then don't fret. Have yourself a good cry, address your feelings and then move along with your life, trusting that Jesus is right beside you.

No one likes to hear that there are "other fish in the sea," especially after seeing the big one get away. But when you have Jesus as the Fisherman, be confident that everything will be okay. Have you ever heard of the Pan Theory? All will pan out in the end.

To be blunt, maybe what you lost in this relationship wasn't really such a loss. Since God wants to be in your life far more than you realize, why not invite him to be your matchmaker?

Linda

In high school I dated a guy who was a year older and basically a decent guy. As the year progressed, however, we became sexually active, and things started falling apart. I heard rumors of his unfaithfulness, and eventually he broke up with me. I was totally crushed. I had invested my entire being in this fragile relationship.

In reality, it wasn't so much the loss of love that scared me; it was the thought of being without a date to rescue me from the mundane reality of family life. I dreaded having to remain at home on weekends while the entire high school, or so it seemed, was out having a good time. Consequently, within a few weeks I fell into another empty and unprofitable relationship. It seemed to me that a bad relationship was better than none at all.

Now that I am older and more self-possessed, I understand that a lack of self-worth led me to sacrifice myself on the altar of dating. I was willing to devalue myself for the sake of appearing normal. I thought that something was wrong with people who didn't have dates, like maybe no one wanted to date them. Now I realize that my standard was barely a standard at all.

You do yourself a disservice and even some harm if you stay in an unhealthy relationship for fear of what others might think or to avoid staying home and learning how to enjoy time alone or with your family. What God thinks of you is more important than what a few peers think. Actually, these peers are probably as full of insecurity and anxiety as you. No young person has it all together when it comes to being hip and dealing with relationships. Everyone struggles through the same thoughts and questions.

Give yourself the best gift of all: ask God's help in discerning which relationships are worth your time and effort and which are not. Set your standards high, and don't fear that you will never date again. God wants the best for you, and he'll put the best in your path when the time is right.

Until then you don't have to be unsociable. Invest in good friendships. Invest in your relationship with God. Find activities that you enjoy, such as sports or dancing, and invest time in those. You'll become well-rounded, interesting and more prepared for that special relationship when it does come your way.

No-Nos for Breaking Up: What Not to Do

Relay your decision through a friend.

Send a note.

Spread rumors or lies about the ex.

Say spiteful things.

Lead the person on only to make a clean break.

Ignore the person.

Force mutual friends to pick sides.

Keep your feelings hidden inside.

Seek only peer advice.

Exclude God from the decision.

Question: *Is it OK to date someone special, or are we supposed to be "just friends"?*

Chris

For starters, you should *at least* be friends. If you have little in common with someone beyond physical experimentation, then you have a significant problem. Growing in your relationship together can eventually take you beyond "just friends." This can be a proper leading toward your future vocation, or it can be a path in the wrong direction. It's up to you to set the course.

Ask yourself what your parents' thoughts are on dating. What standards have they set, and what are they expecting from you? If they have provided no guidelines or if parental involvement in your relationships is limited, then you have to have your head on straight in order to battle peer pressure and the temptations of premarital sex.

Here is a helpful hint: the moment you find yourself more interested in sexual gratification than in the person is the moment you need to step back and take a break. Having feelings that are more than basic friendship is natural, but trying not to satisfy those feelings can be difficult.

Be careful about where your relationship is heading. The step past friendship can be a massive one. Being committed to someone, wanting to invest in your relationship, is fine, but in our culture the next step after "just friends" is most often the step into sexual intimacy.

New levels of friendship shouldn't include sacrificing morality.

Instead, develop your friendship on as many levels as possible. Even married couples need to continue to develop their friendship in order to foster their relationship. If you are going to spend the rest of your lives together, you will want to have something to talk about when you aren't "doing it"—which, ladies and gentlemen, is far more time than you think. Pursue intellectual, social and spiritual interests together, and discuss your dreams and aspirations.

It comes down to this: what do you really want from a date? Do you want to go beyond basic friendship for reasons other than sexual intimacy? If so, will your relationship then need to advance somehow in a month or two? In other words, how fast are you moving? Is your speed appropriate to your life situation? Are you in a position to seriously discuss marriage?

In short, move slowly in developing this friendship. Enjoy getting to know the person you feel drawn to. And let God lead you.

Linda

Being "just friends" is not a lower level of existence. There are far too many married couples who have the right to engage in sex whenever they want but lack a true relationship founded on friendship. How does this happen?

When couples start out focused on romance, the bond of simple friendship has little chance to develop. Then, when the demands and busyness of married life settle in, it becomes easy for the husband and wife to just coexist, put no effort into developing their love and take each other for granted. Every marriage goes through difficult phases, but it's unfortunate when a couple is stuck in this awful existence.

To begin a dating experience as "just friends" is a blessing. If the two of you have a good time hanging around together, especially in a group environment, and engage in good conversation, then you are farther along than many of the couples you consider serious dating items. If this good friendship develops but nothing more comes of it, then at least you've gained a friend.

Avoiding sexual promiscuity also avoids the potential of a broken heart. You can leave the relationship in God's hands, which is a good place for it to be.

You will never regret being unhurried in a relationship. On the other hand, a relationship that moves too fast often brings regret.

A Memory Moment

Linda

I had lived in the oppressively hot and muggy state of Florida since I was five, and Chris since he was sixteen. No matter how long you live there, you never get used to

things like the winter traffic, the summer heat, mosqui-
toes the size of small planes and sand everywhere. On the
plus side, Florida has beautiful winters, year-round water
sports and Disney World.

As seniors in high school, Chris and I participated in
Grad Nite. This is when Disney World shuts its gates to the
public and allows in only the seniors of Florida high
schools. We were free to roam during the ridiculous hours
of 11 P.M. to 5 A.M.

Chris and I were geared up for this exciting evening.
As was my ritual, I took two hours to get ready. I wore my
favorite dress and curled my hair. Chris even wore a tie.

We arrived at the park after the three-hour bus trip
and were herded through the gates along with hundreds of
other seniors. So far, the evening seemed ideal and
romantic. We boarded the ferry that glides across the
large lake to the main street of the Magic Kingdom.

As Chris and I stood at the railing of the boat, looking
at the peaceful water and feeling the gentle breeze, it
started to pour. This was not the average Florida drizzle
but a torrent that conjured up images of Noah's flood.

We left the ferry and ran for cover, but already we
were soaked to the skin. The rain flooded corridors with
several inches of water. We took off our shoes as we tried
to make our way to the roller coasters.

Neither Chris nor I had come prepared with a rain-
coat or umbrella, but after half an hour of frustration, we
noticed other students wearing clear rain ponchos. They

told us that the gift shops were selling them, so we hurried over and each purchased one. So much for looking good!

Eventually the rain stopped, but the damage was done. Our clothes were completely wet, our shoes were soggy, and my nicely curled hair was flat. By this time it was after midnight, and the rain had cooled the air. We began to feel chilled in our wet clothes.

We thought the smartest thing was to keep the raincoats on to preserve warmth but that didn't help. In retrospect, I realize we should have removed the ponchos and allowed our clothes to dry. But noooo—we stayed wet the entire six hours. Most of the rides were air-conditioned, and I nearly froze on Mr. Toad's Wild Ride. Somehow we did manage to laugh and enjoy ourselves.

Comfort finally came on the way home. We changed out of our wet clothes and into the Grad Nite shirts we had purchased on our way to the bus. I felt a little disappointed about the evening, but I knew we had made a memory that my children would hear about someday.

What Do You Think?

Write your answers to the following questions in your personal journal.

1. Would you consider yourself to be someone who has a relationship with God? (If not, contact a leader in your church, or find a Christian group with which you feel comfortable.)

2. Unconfessed sin has power; it leaves you vulnerable to greater sin. Are there any acts, words or thoughts you want to acknowledge and ask God's forgiveness for?

3. Take a long look at your wardrobe. Is a change in your choice of clothing in order?

4. Is the relationship you are in one that God would consider honorable?

5. Have you hurt someone by your behavior or attitude while dating or during a break-up? How can you make restitution and bring healing?

Thoughts to Consider

Yeah, if a girl is looking good and she knows it, and she's putting it on display, it's tough not to chomp on the bait. Here's what you do: Just thank God for his good work, breathe, and keep walking straight ahead. Look her in the eye if you're talking to her. Treat her like a lady, even if she's asking for something else. (*Catholic Teen Survival Guide: Love and Dating*)[2]

If you're one of those guys who show off his body to impress the ladies, stop being such a Hollywood wannabe. Humble yourself a bit. (*Catholic Teen Survival Guide: Love and Dating*)[3]

Relationships do not come in a plastic wrapper, in a three-pack, in tutti-frutti flavors, with ribs, multi-colored, on a lollipop stick, in "glow-in-the-dark" or dangling on earrings or on key chains. Real relationships come with hard work, self-sacrifice, and fidelity. (Dr. John R. Diggs, Jr., "Are Condoms Better than Nothing?")[4]

Whatever is true, whatever is honorable, whatever is just, whatever is pure, whatever is pleasing, whatever is commendable, if there is any excellence and if there is anything worthy of praise, think about these things. (Philippians 4:8)

Above all, clothe yourselves with love, which binds everything together in perfect harmony. And let the peace of Christ rule in your hearts, to which indeed you were called in the one body. And be thankful. Let the word of Christ dwell in you richly; teach and admonish one another in all wisdom; and with gratitude in your hearts sing psalms, hymns, and spiritual songs to God. And whatever you do, in word or deed, do everything in the name of the Lord Jesus, giving thanks to God the Father through him. (Colossians 3:14–17)

Section Four

Hard Questions

Well, we've answered lots of questions so far. Here are some that you might feel less free to ask because of their personal nature.

We're also including here more great memory moments from "The Chris and Linda Story," as well as more dating tips. So keep going!

Question: *Am I still a virgin if I have oral sex? Anal sex?*

Chris and Linda

The *American Heritage Dictionary* defines *virginity* as "being a virgin; chastity; the state of being pure, unsullied or untouched." In the strictest sense of the word, a virgin is one who has not had sexual intercourse. But let's consider some of the broader issues that underlie these questions.

Virginity is part of a bigger picture, the life of chastity. All Christians are called to be chaste, whether married or single. In other words, we are all expected to control our sexual thoughts and actions and to engage in sex only within marriage. Even there it isn't true that anything goes. For example, it is just as sinful for married people to masturbate or to use pornography as it is for single people.

Chastity has to do with the right ordering of our sexual desires; it encompasses virginity. Virginity is more

NOT READY FOR MARRIAGE, NOT READY FOR SEX

than a physical term, therefore; it is a state of the heart. People who participate in oral or anal sex without actually "hitting the bulls-eye" have little concern about being chaste and pure. They are not virgins.

Consider the reality of oral and anal sex: these are selfish acts concerned primarily with sexual stimulation and gratification. They are incapable of bringing about new life. Of course, this is the very reason young people engage in these practices, but stripping sex of its life-giving property warps the intent of God. He made sex to be unitive and procreative: it brings two married people together in a fun and unifying activity that might result in a baby.

Consider also the fact that oral or anal sex will probably lead to vaginal intercourse. It's the logical next step. In other words, the moral slide doesn't stop.

One more thing: oral and anal sex leave you open to contracting many sexually transmitted diseases. HIV, the virus that causes AIDS, is very efficiently passed through anal intercourse. Among many other problems, oral intercourse can result in a lifelong contagious disease such as herpes of the mouth. Imagine telling your future spouse that you have herpes but, hey, don't worry, because technically you're still a virgin. It doesn't jibe, does it? Keep in mind that these are called oral and anal *sex* for a reason.

As to virginity, most of you have probably heard the expression "secondary virginity." The term refers to being previously sexually active outside of marriage but rededicating oneself to a chaste lifestyle. This was the case with us when we finally freed ourselves from the weight of sexual sin and remained pure for the two years before we married. Our wedding night was not the same as for those who had never had sex, but it was a beautiful experience that expressed the emotions and healing that came with chastity. Secondary virginity can heal many wounds.

A Quick Memory Moment

Linda

Chris and I were walking through a dorm parking lot together when Chris saw a ketchup packet on the ground. He decided to try an old trick, and he stomped on it in order to squirt the contents across the pavement. Instead of hitting the ground, however, the ketchup splattered on the leg of my favorite pants. He looked at me with fear in his eyes, bracing himself for my wrath, but we had a good laugh instead.

Question: *Is masturbation OK?*

Chris

As a young man I wanted to masturbate (please notice the past tense). Well, that is only half true, because even though I wanted the forthcoming pleasure, I hated the guilt that accompanied it. And as much as I tried to justify my actions, I could not escape the feeling of having just sinned.

My father once asked me if I ever masturbated, and I said yes. He told me that I shouldn't feel guilty, since it was a natural act. His endorsement was exactly what I wanted to hear, yet it brought only momentary relief. I still felt instinctively that masturbation was wrong.

Once my sister and I were at an airport with my father, and I shuffled over to the magazine rack while my dad looked at something else. There, within my preteen reach, was a pornographic magazine. My father caught me sneaking a peak at its glossy contents. I was horrified at having been caught red-handed. He calmly said that there was nothing wrong with looking at the human anatomy, but in most of those magazines the women were not portrayed honestly and the photography wasn't really art.

Not wanting to stir the spark into a flame, I withheld my comment: I wasn't looking at those photos to enjoy their artistic value, and I didn't care if the women were modified. I looked because I liked what I saw.

The differences in belief between my divorced parents were blatant in such matters. In my mother's house I would never have spoken about masturbation or the artistic aspects of nudity. I do recall her indicating that masturbation was not acceptable, regardless of natural inclinations. Even though most boys my age did it, this didn't make it right. If my friends jumped off a cliff, would I do the same? Certainly not! My mother loved to use that expression.

So I endured the guilt as I continued to practice something that made me feel great and awful at the same time. Repeatedly I repented, but failure was always just around the corner.

Visits to the photography section of bookstores fed the seed. *National Geographic* offered some visual stimulation, while pornographic magazines were a major draw. Unfortunately, some of my friends' parents had these stashed in not-so-secret locations in their homes. Watching a movie with nudity also stirred the passions that were gaining greater control of my life. I know some people masturbate just to relieve tension, without thinking pornographic thoughts, but attempting the act without engaging the imagination isn't easy.

For a while I felt that I had no control over this area of my life. My flesh warred against my spirit; in my heart I longed to stop. Why did I feel that this act was so wrong? I didn't understand that my actions were selfish, and I didn't even have any deeply spiritual motivation. What I did have was an internal comprehension that sex was part of something that was meant for a later time and a different manner. It wasn't meant to be a solitary experience.

One day, while contemplating the struggle I had with masturbation, I realized that even though I didn't want to sin in this way, deep within I wanted to sin *in just this way*. I was able to discern the internal and definite choice I made in submitting to this temptation over time. The result of this clarity was that I honestly began to try to change some of the thought habits I had developed.

Change was difficult. Many movies and the pictures and even the articles in pornographic magazines stayed lodged in my mind with precise clarity, regardless of how much I grew spiritually. I couldn't shake some of the images and the memory of what I had participated in. The habit of masturbation was the result of not winning the battles with these thoughts for quite a long time.

The war I fought with masturbation was similar to the one I fought with premarital sex. I wanted to do the right thing, but I wanted to fulfill fleshly desires too. Was there victory? Absolutely, and praise God for it! And not just for me either. Many people have chosen Christ intentionally over self-gratification.

Breaking strongholds in our lives is not easy, especially if we habitually deny ourselves the grace of the sacraments. The fact that I didn't grow up Catholic doesn't give me any excuses, but I do feel the opportunities afforded Catholics within the sacraments of reconciliation and the Eucharist are not incidental to the fight for chastity. Remember, not only are our sins forgiven in the confessional, but we also receive the grace there to say no to temptation. Take advantage of the graces of the sacraments.

When you fall in regard to this sin, don't get angry with yourself or fall prey to anxiety. Get to confession, repent and start over; continue to do this until you achieve victory. Find a friend or mentor who will hold you accountable for your behavior. Block access to pornographic sites on your computer. Consider getting profes-sional counseling if you find yourself in the grip of Internet porn.

In many ways we come back to the question, what do you really want? If you crave self-gratification then you will stir your passions with cyber porn, magazines, movies or sketchy opportunities to participate in sinful acts. If you desire Christ, you will repent and turn from the direction in which you are heading.

Linda

When we think of masturbation, we generally think of men, since more men than women seem to struggle with the issue. But women too can get caught in this practice. And whether we're talking about male or female, the truth about masturbation remains consistent.

One afternoon I heard Chris on the phone discussing his thinking about masturbation. The woman he was talk-ing with considered Chris's stance overly stringent; she saw physical exploration as natural. True, it is natural for kids to discover their bodies and explore them, but we're talking about young adults, not two-year-olds. There is a difference between a young child's finding out how his or her body works and an adult's participation in a lustful and selfish activity on a regular basis.

What makes this "natural" release wrong?

• The *Catechism of the Catholic Church* points out that the church has constantly maintained that masturbation is "intrinsically and gravely disordered." Quoting the Congregation for the Doctrine of the Faith, it continues: "The deliberate use of the sexual faculty, for whatever reason, outside of marriage is essentially contrary to its purpose" (*CCC* #2352).

• The sexual act is meant to be both pleasurable—fostering the relationship of the couple—and open to the creation of new life. In other words, it is unitive and procreative. The gift of sex and orgasm is for married *partners*. It is meant to be shared in love and commitment with a spouse for life. Marriage creates a safe haven for a couple and their children, and sex plays a part in fostering the love and respect a husband and wife have for each other.

• There is nothing mutually self-giving about masturbation. It is a solitary act. When it becomes a habit, it powerfully reinforces emotional and psychological isolation. Far from being soothing and normal, as many people claim, it is a lonely act that imprisons the person inside himself.

• Further, the habitual practice of masturbation can make it difficult to enjoy normal sexual relations when the time comes for marriage: Masturbation has taught you what you like and taught you to focus on yourself. Sex in marriage really is about the other person, caring for and thinking about your partner first. Masturbation allows you to avoid the reality that relationships take work and that sex is *always* meant to be part of a relationship.

- The practice of masturbation can be considered a form of infidelity when practiced in marriage. It can create serious problems in the sexual life of the couple. If you develop the habit prior to marriage, you will probably have a difficult time breaking it afterward.
- Finally, the gospel calls us to high standards regarding purity. Jesus said: "You have heard that it was said, 'You shall not commit adultery.' But I say to you that everyone who looks at a woman with lust has already committed adultery with her in his heart" (Matthew 5:27–28).
- It is impossible to masturbate successfully while dwelling on spiritual matters. We Christians are called to set our minds on things above (see Colossians 3:2) and to have the mind of Christ (see Philippians 2:5). Masturbation is saturated with lust. God has better plans for your thought life.

> Do not be conformed to this world, but be transformed by the renewing of your minds, so that you may discern what is the will of God—what is good and acceptable and perfect (Romans 12:2).

Thought to Consider

Pornography is a hard addiction to overcome. It's not going to go away by itself. Sexual sin can be just as addictive as drugs, if not more so. You have to pull it out by its roots. (*Catholic Teen Survival Guide: Love and Dating*)[1]

A Quick Memory Moment

Linda

Sometimes on our dates Chris and I would take a small amount of money and blow it totally on each other. I emphasize "small," since college students are usually broke.

We would head to the mall, split up and find items representing our love for each other. We'd return at a specified time bearing the surprise presents to exchange. Once we handed each other the exact same gift: a wind-up pair of moving red lips that you could pin to a jacket.

The most memorable occasion was when Chris returned with a pair of white baby shoes for me. We were at the point in our relationship when marriage was a serious consideration. I saved those shoes, and when our first daughter, Hannah, was an infant, she wore them. To this day they hang on the headboard of our bed as a tribute to the memories we have shared during our years together.

Question: *Why is it wrong for me to have sex? It is natural, and everybody else is doing it.*

Chris and Linda

The funny thing about a lot of these questions is that most of you already know the answers to them. Deep down inside you know the truth, though you may find it disappointing that you can't justify sexual intimacy outside of marriage.

You also know that not "everybody" is doing it. Even if they were, that wouldn't make it right. Would you jump off a cliff if everybody were doing that too? We're back at that cliff. Just because everyone is doing something doesn't make it right.

The right time for sex is in the safety of marriage. Why is it safe there? The answer falls roughly into two categories: the relational and the physical.

Relational: The first and perhaps most significant effect of sex outside of marriage is that it damages our relationship with God. When we use sex in a way other than he intended, we disobey him by breaking his clear and specific rules. We place ourselves outside his will, we break faith with him, and we say, in essence, that we don't trust him. It's as simple as that.

When our relationship with God flounders, we open ourselves up to hearing and succumbing to the voices of the culture and of the evil one. It becomes harder to hear God and to receive his love, mercy and direction. A good relationship with God is the foundation for the unfolding of sex within marriage.

Within the confines of marriage, sex acts as a renewal of the covenant between husband and wife. It is a reflection of God's own total and permanent commitment to his people, the church. Marriage is a sacrament and is holy and lifelong. It is a sign of God's faithfulness to us in good times and bad. Within this haven of permanence and trust, sex is safe, protected, nourishing and life-giving.

There is no better sex than married sex, and there should be no sex *but* married sex. Anything less is impermanent and misdirected by its very nature.

Today premarital sexual intimacy is practically considered a rite of passage. People regard sex as a right, as little more than a means to get to know someone or to pass the time or to show a little affection. There are many negative consequences to this attitude, but consider this one: When you have sex with someone outside of marriage, you are contributing to their spiritual darkness.

Jesus said, "Occasions for stumbling are bound to come, but woe to the one by whom the stumbling block comes" (Matthew 18:7). He goes so far as to say that for those who cause the innocent to sin, "it would be better for you if a great millstone were fastened around your neck and you were drowned in the depth of the sea" (Matthew 18:6).

What if the person you are dating is called to be the next Mother Teresa or Pope John Paul II? What if he or she is not becoming who God intended because the sins you engage in together are destroying the hope that once seemed unquenchable? Obviously, we all make our own choices and we can't be blamed for the sin of another, but we can contribute to or create the circumstances that lead another to sin.

A friend of ours told us that when he was in college, a young and beautiful fellow student invited him to have sex. He declined her offer. He wanted this woman to be all that she was meant to be, and he refused to allow her to lower herself for momentary satisfaction. She left in a huff.

Years later he saw this same woman accompanied by a really big man. They approached him, and for a moment our friend feared that the guy was going to crush him. Instead the man shook his hand and thanked him for his integrity toward the woman who was now his wife. His refusal of her come-on had led her to realize that she wasn't a piece of meat but a child of God, worthy of respect.

Finally, a lot of people these days are just sleeping around, but some are practicing what has become known as "serial monogamy." They have sex with the one person they are dating or living with until that relationship breaks down. They then move on to another relationship. They think of themselves as faithful because they generally aren't having sex with anyone but their current partner. But here's what they're learning: how to pack up and go when things get tough or the situation doesn't suit them anymore.

In other words, they're practicing the habit of divorce. Young people sometimes worry about the potential for their future marriage to end in divorce. One way they can prevent that is by refraining from sex until marriage and training themselves now in habits of self-control and self-sacrifice, which will help them weather the rough patches that come to all marriages.

Physical: Sex is natural and good and meant to be completely enjoyable. But just as with every good thing—

money, success or even chocolate cake—humans have a tendency to become selfish with sex. Then it can be hazardous.

People get hurt emotionally and psychologically as they go from partner to partner. Married people sometimes give themselves over to adultery, leaving broken families in their wake. Sexual abuse, unintended pregnancies and the horror of abortion are all evident in our free-wheeling, sexually corrupt culture.

The epidemic of sexually transmitted diseases in this country makes clear the physical damage inflicted by extramarital sex. Sometimes these diseases have no symptoms and so do their damage before they are detected. Chlamydia, for example, can lead to pelvic inflammatory disease (PID), which can cause infertility, chronic pelvic pain and other serious consequences. According to the Centers for Disease Control and prevention, three million people are infected with chlamydia each year. Every year in the United States more than a hundred thousand women become infertile as a result of PID.[2] Some STDs, such as genital herpes and AIDS, are incurable, and the latter is fatal.

So if your special someone starts to whisper sweet nothings in your ear in the hope of landing you in bed, here's what you can whisper back: chlamydia, gonorrhea, HIV, genital warts, herpes, hepatitis, syphilis...Well, you get the picture. Not one of these diseases is worth that momentary pleasure or that tempting relationship.

THOUGHTS TO CONSIDER

If someone were absolutely "dead set" on killing himself, and there was nothing you could do to change his mind, would you show him the best spot on the bridge to jump from?...Sex outside marriage is similar. If someone is "dead set" on doing it, he's dead set on doing something that puts him at significant physical, emotional and spiritual risk. (Mary Beth Bonacci, *Real Love*)[3]

In the kingdom of God, the Lord tells His people, "Be holy, for I am holy." Our culture tells us, "If it feels good, do it." One of these two kingdoms must fall, and we must, by word and action, choose which side we are on. (Josh McDowell and Dick Day, *Why Wait?*)[4]

True love is doing what's best for the beloved. This is what chastity is all about. It's putting someone else before yourself. (*Catholic Teen Survival Guide: Love and Dating*)[5]

God *always* forgives, man *sometimes* forgives; but Nature *never* forgives. (An old saying)

HPV [human papilloma virus] is remarkably contagious. Statistically, college students will almost certainly be infected after having sex with four different people. (John R. Diggs, Jr., "Human Papilloma Virus")[6]

The most important risk factor for cervical cancer is infection by the human papilloma virus (HPV).[7]

A Quick Memory Moment

Chris

Linda decided to teach me karate, an ancient art at which she excelled. I obtained a uniform, and we had classes in my backyard. After several weeks of practice I was promoted from white belt to yellow and moved on to more difficult skills.

In order to critique my moves, Linda took pictures of my mistakes. I'm not too fond of those pictures, but that doesn't matter. The time together and the memories are what made the experience important.

Question: *I can use the pill and not get pregnant, and no one will ever know, right?*

Linda

It is estimated that more than fifty percent of sexually active teenage girls are on chemical contraceptives; most of these use the pill, and the remainder use some type of patch.[8] The pill is designed to prevent pregnancy, but it does so at some risk. All variations of the birth control pill work in one of three ways: by preventing ovulation, by altering the mucus in the cervix or by changing the lining of the uterus so that it cannot support a fertilized egg.

Most commonly the pill prevents ovulation. Ovulation is the release of an egg from the ovary. If ovulation doesn't take place, there is no egg to be fertilized, and a woman cannot get pregnant.

Although the pill is designed to prevent ovulation, it doesn't always do so.[9] "Breakthrough ovulation" is more likely to occur with the newer pill, which contains a lower dose of estrogen, or when the pill is not taken properly or is mixed with other medications.

The pill also works by thickening the mucus around the cervix to prevent sperm from getting to an egg. Still, if a woman on the pill does ovulate and has sexual intercourse, some sperm may pass through the cervix and fertilize the egg, and she can become pregnant.

The third function of the pill comes into play here. It alters the lining of the uterus, making it inhospitable to the fertilized egg and preventing the egg from implanting. This fertilized egg—a new human being—is then flushed out of the body during menstrual bleeding.

At least on some occasions, then, the pill works by aborting a baby. For this reason it is considered an abortifacient. The church forbids its use, as it does the use of all artificial contraceptives.

The Couple to Couple League notes that "many otherwise pro-life physicians and pharmacists find it hard to admit that these abortifacient properties exist because they would have to discontinue prescribing and dispensing the pill if they were to remain consistent in their respect for life at all its stages of development."[10] It's hard to avoid this fact, though, since it is plainly stated, among other places, in the *Physicians' Desk Reference*, the reference book all medical doctors use for information when prescribing drugs: the pill causes "changes in...the endrometrium [the lining of the uterus] (which reduce the likelihood of implantation)," resulting in the death of the fertilized egg.[11]

The pill is a powerful hormonal cocktail and does have side effects. These include breast cancer, stroke and heart attack. Furthermore, birth control pills offer no protection from sexually transmitted diseases, and a woman engaging in illicit intercourse has a greater risk of contracting a sexually transmitted disease than of getting pregnant. No contraceptive is guaranteed to prevent the spread of disease, not even a condom.

Approximately three million teens contract an STD every year.[12] People who are sexually active outside the bounds of marriage put their own health and the health of future children at grave risk.

Abstaining from all sexual relations is the only way to be 100-percent certain of avoiding pregnancy and STDs. And yes, you can get pregnant through genital contact even if there is no penetration of the vagina.

Question: *I'm pregnant. What now?*

Linda

The few weeks before I met Chris were the worst of my life. My morals had hit rock bottom, and I thought I was pregnant. My cycle was always regular, and that month I was late.

I told the boy involved, and we arrived at a solution that was contrary to my entire upbringing. I grew up in a Christian home and knew right from wrong. But I felt I couldn't face my parents if, in fact, I was pregnant. The boy agreed to fund an abortion. That seemed like the only choice.

In the darkness of that moment I could still recognize how a series of bad decisions had led to an even worse one. I had never thought that I would find myself in that situation. It was a surreal moment; I didn't feel like myself. How could I consider killing my baby? I was full of shame.

To my great relief I was not pregnant. So unlike many women— there have been over forty-six million abortions in the United States since 1973—I never faced an unexpected pregnancy. I came to realize, though, that even people who are raised in a Christian atmosphere can throw conviction and logic out the window when faced with tough circumstances.

Many of us who have grown up in the church let the sermons, homilies, books and tapes about premarital sex slide by as bits of general information. We don't think these issues affect people like us. We hear stories about this or that couple who had an abortion, but it all seems so distant, even if it occurs in our own school or youth group.

Things change when it is you. Then you look at these issues from a perspective of panic. That, of course, is not the best way to tackle such a monumental moment.

In this time of decision, let me say unequivocally, *don't even consider abortion.* Why? Because even though you have made a mistake, a new life is planted divinely within you. Life begins at conception, and your baby, the recipient of God's breath of life, is waiting to reflect a God who is bigger than your mistakes. This child within you not only has gifts and talents to someday place at the service of humanity, but he or she also has a soul. Your child will live forever, having been created in God's image.

Not only would abortion destroy the life of that child, but it would also leave you with lifelong regret and the potential for serious depression. Keep in mind, too, the physical side effects that can result from abortion, including infertility, infection and even maternal death.

So you regret your mistake? Don't further your sin by adding abortion, the murder of your child, to promiscuity. Don't let fear drive you to take the gift of this life.

So you can't stand the father of the child? That too is no reason to destroy the life within you. And there is no turning back from the truth that you carry a new human life. You—and the man involved—are already parents. Your life will never be the same.

Of course you want to avoid the humiliation and the disappointment that pregnancy will cause your parents. You want to continue your life the way it was, but instead you are being called to embrace the opportunity to grow, to mature and to make decisions that will support this new life.

If you feel that you can't talk to your parents, then find a teacher, youth group leader, parent of a friend, relative or other individual whom you know is pro-life. That person can help you approach your parents with the news.

Contact your church or your local crisis pregnancy center for help with pre- and postnatal care and basic needs. (Avoid Planned Parenthood, which is in the business of ending pregnancy, and other pro-abortion centers.)

This unexpected pregnancy might be the most difficult situation you will ever have to face. It may seem overwhelming, but there are people who will help you move forward confidently, with courage and strength. Find the resources you need to help you and your baby survive.

And remember that God truly loves you and your baby. He knows your struggles, and he will help you. These words from Psalm 23 are yours to claim: "Even though I walk through the darkest valley, / I fear no evil; / for you are with me; / your rod and your staff—/ they comfort me" (Psalm 23:4).

Chris

The first time I was pregnant…Well, actually, I never was pregnant. After all, I'm a male and it is biologically impossible for me to bear a child. There have been times, though, when the possibility of fatherhood came a bit too close for comfort. I'm not sure why I was spared this, because my actions didn't reflect virtue.

There were girls in my high school who were pregnant, though this was not common. There was even one young woman who walked around campus the full nine months, getting bigger and bigger before all. In retrospect I realize that this was pretty gutsy back in the eighties. In today's high schools it's not uncommon to find a day-care center located within the school for the benefit of teenage parents.

So what about you? Are you one of those who could have been a father any number of times? You probably know other young people who have had babies and some who have had abortions. Have you learned anything from seeing the consequences of their choices? If you can learn from another's mistake and make the choice for integrity, you're a wise man. I applaud you.

Perhaps you have fathered a child far sooner than you imagined you would. If so, have you participated in procuring an abortion? Or did you evade your responsibility to the woman who carried your child in other ways, not standing by her emotionally and financially, for example? Did you get married and now, as a young dad, find yourself overwhelmed?

If you have helped in any way to procure an abortion, now is the time to get to confession, repent and be reconciled to Christ. He is bigger than your mistakes.

If you just discovered that you are a father, abortion is not the answer. Two wrongs won't do anything here but wound all involved. Nor can you ignore what has happened either since you are just as responsible for this pregnancy as your partner is.

Recently I talked with a man who works with disadvantaged young people in poverty-stricken sections of Brooklyn. He had been mentoring a girl who had come a long way in her spiritual journey. Her life was hard but not unusually so, given her circumstances.

One day, as she chatted with him, the conversation became awkward and forced. The man sensed that something was wrong. He had begun to suspect that the girl was pregnant.

In fact, she was pregnant, and she finally admitted it. She had been afraid to tell him because she didn't want to disappoint this man who had been like a father to her or face what she assumed would be his angry response.

To her surprise, her mentor responded with joy. He said, "Wow, a new and beautiful life. What a grace you have been given!"

She looked at him and said, "I thought you'd be mad at me."

He responded, "How can I be mad? This is a new life, a new child, a beautiful gift from an amazing God.

Honestly, your timing is horrible, and I mean horrible, but this new life is a cause for celebration."

I was struck by the grace God gave this man in his response. He wasn't condoning her actions; he was looking past them to focus on the critical fact of new life. He didn't live in a dream world but in a very unglamorous part of New York. Instead of heaping more condemnation upon a young woman who encountered little else from society, he found God's hand in the situation and recognized the beauty amid the chaos.

We should always celebrate new life, even as we recognize that the circumstances we face pose challenges. Let's not overlook the gifts God gives. He is so much bigger than our sin.

So you were only trying to have some fun! You never meant to create a child. There will certainly be adjustments, struggles, frustrations and a steeper hill to climb, but you have been blessed with the miracle of life. This child, in some ways, is a physical expression of the new life that God desires to bring to birth in you, regardless of your sin.

Your timing too is horrible, but God will give you the grace to persevere. Also remember that if you are not in a position to raise this child, there are countless families who long to adopt. Your baby could be the answer to many prayers.

Don't panic; have nothing to do with abortion. As many will tell you who have made that choice, out of sight is *not* out of mind.

THOUGHT TO CONSIDER

Human life must be respected and protected absolutely from the moment of conception. From the first moment of his existence, a human being must be recognized as having the rights of a person. (*CCC* #2270)

ANOTHER MEMORY MOMENT

Linda

Chris and I decided to make dinner together. We went to the grocery store and stared at the wide selection of meats, feeling confused and overwhelmed. We had never bought our own steak before, so we guessed at what would be good. Then we picked up some Hamburger Helper.

We went to Chris's house and began to cook, only to discover that we had forgotten to buy hamburger. I don't remember what we thought we were going to do with steak and Hamburger Helper, since even the name on the box gives you a clue to the key ingredient. We were new to this.

Chris's mom stepped in and informed us that we had purchased round steak, a tough cut of beef that requires a fair amount of preparation. She then demonstrated how to cook it, first pounding it in order to flatten the meat and tenderize it, then flouring and seasoning it and finally sautéing it in oil. In the end it was actually Chris's mom who prepared the meal.

Question: *I am a victim of date rape. How can I prevent this from happening again, and what does God think of me now?*

Chris and Linda

Date rape is forced sex between two people who know each other, if only slightly. It involves someone you think of as a friend, a friend of a friend, an acquaintance or a date.

When a woman says no to sex but the man persists, he is guilty of rape and can be convicted. *No* means no; it's as simple as that. Men can be victims of date rape, but this is uncommon.

There are drugs, known as "date rape" drugs, that when slipped into someone's drink render him or her unconscious and open to rape. The man who dopes a woman's drink and forces sex on her has committed a criminal offense.

Various factors lead a person to cross the line of acceptable behavior and force sex on another. For some it might be movies, TV programs or music lyrics that glorify violent behavior as cool or exciting. For others it might be peer pressure or simply a weak moment.

Some guys feel they "deserve" to go all the way because of "signals" they receive, even if those signals are all in their minds. Some guys come from homes where domestic violence is common. Some people are just screwed up as a result of other circumstances.

If you have been sexually assaulted in a date scenario, it is not your fault, no matter what led up to this violent act. The rapist—for that is what he is even if he is a fellow student or a coworker or a friend of your roommate—is always accountable for surrendering his self-control and assaulting you. His excuses are meaningless. You are the victim here, in God's eyes and the eyes of the law.

I hope you sought medical attention immediately and that you reported the crime to the police. If not, do so as soon as possible. Although this may be uncomfortable for you, it is important that the rapist be held accountable for his crime. You may be able to prevent his harming others.

Talk to your parents or another trusted adult. You may want to seek professional help; if so, consult a therapist who shares a Christian perspective. Counseling will help you restore trust and recover a healthy view of relationships. Pray that God brings healing to your spirit, and ask him to help you forgive the assailant.

There are ways to protect yourself from date rape in the future:

- Postpone dating a person until you have known him for a while in a variety of situations.
- Go out in groups. Having other people present protects you from unwanted advances.
- Choose the location of your date wisely. Questionable locations will lead to questionable behavior. Dark places without supervision, unwholesome parties and other compromising locations are not good choices.

- Avoid alcohol, and stay away from drugs. Many experts suggest that women handle their own drinks at parties or other gatherings and that they refuse any drink that they have left unattended.
- If you find yourself pressured for sex, say no in a way that makes it clear you mean it.
- Remember that the ways you dress, behave and talk send messages that might be interpreted in ways you don't intend. Ask yourself, "Would Jesus be pleased with the way I am dressing, acting and speaking?"
- Finally, trust your instincts. If you feel uneasy, get out before it's too late.

A person who sincerely cares about his date will accept her decision to refuse sex. If your date seems resentful, that is a warning to avoid any further investment in a relationship that could have devastating consequences.

Thoughts to Consider

If date rape happens to you:
- Remember...you are not to blame.
- Get help immediately.
- Get medical attention as soon as possible. Do not shower, wash, douche or change your clothes. Valuable evidence could be destroyed.
- Get counseling to help you through the recovery process. Rape is a traumatic experience, and trained counselors can make recovery easier and quicker.[13]

A Memory Moment of a Lifetime

Linda

Chris and his friend Tony planned to take Teresa, my roommate, and me out for a date one particular evening. They told us to dress nicely because, unlike so many of our ramblings, this would be an actual date, one that consisted of a plan.

The guys picked us up, and then we seemed to drive for quite a while. We ended up at a popular Italian restaurant in an unfamiliar part of West Palm Beach. As we got out of the car, the guys pulled out a camera, and each couple posed for a few shots.

The hostess seated us in the back, and we ordered our meal. It was a pleasant evening, the food was great, and as usual, the four of us had a good time. The only crazy thing was that Tony and Chris would occasionally jump up from the table, rush to the corner of the room and hold a brief meeting. We assumed they were working out the plans for the night. Since such sporadic conferences were normal for our dates, Teresa and I thought nothing of it.

At the end of the meal we heard clapping and singing heading our way. I thought the guys had told the waitress that it was one of our birthdays. The staff placed a cake on the table and started singing. Confusion mounted as I realized that they were singing "Congratulations," not "Happy Birthday."

I tried to get a look at the cake to see what it said. As I leaned over the table, I noticed that Tony was kneeling down in front of Teresa. Slowly I turned toward Chris. There he was before me on one knee, holding an open ring box. Together the guys asked for our hands in marriage as the entire restaurant looked on. Of course we said yes.

We quickly wrapped up the meal, paid and left as the other diners called "Congratulations." After that we drove to the island of Palm Beach and strolled down the romantically lit streets hand in hand. We took a few more photos as we posed in front of palm trees covered in white lights.

I never had daydreamed about how my future husband would propose to me. The only thing I wanted was to be surprised. I love the memories of that night. And the best part was that Chris blew me away. I never saw it coming.

Question: *How long should you date someone before you move toward marriage?*

Linda
The answer to this question varies considerably. Chris and I dated three and a half years before we married, although we knew we wanted to be together forever almost immediately. Even though we daydreamed about the future, we didn't take serious steps toward marriage or even get engaged until six months before we actually tied the knot.

We had to ask some serious questions: Can we afford the financial responsibilities of marriage? What about finishing our educations? Is this God's timing?

On the other hand, Chris's sister, Carrie, and her husband met, became engaged and were married in eight months. They met in college, however, and they were both holding down good jobs. Billy displayed a spiritual maturity that was lacking in Carrie's former boyfriend, and she knew immediately that he was "the one."

Carrie's previous relationship had lasted for three years. They had discussed marriage, but Carrie thinks they did so simply because they had been together for so long. Just because a couple has spent years together doesn't mean they are supposed to remain together. Sometimes people get comfortable and are blind to the reality that their relationship is outside of God's will.

In general, early marriages can be burdened with problems, and we don't recommend them. Yet we know a great couple who tied the knot shortly after graduation from high school. They had been committed to each other from the beginning of their dating. They both had jobs and were saving for the future. Not only were they able to pay for a lovely ceremony, but they also fully furnished a small house with new furniture without the use of credit. After a year of marriage, just before they turned twenty-one, they purchased their first home.

This couple displayed an unusual amount of maturity and wisdom in their relationship. It is uncommon to find young people so levelheaded about commitment and what it takes to make marriage work. One key factor in their success was the support they received from family. Their parents must have detected their readiness, or they never would have approved of the marriage.

As you can see, every situation is different. But here are some things to consider.

- Age is important whether you want to admit it or not. We acquire wisdom and understanding the older we get and the more we seek God.

- Although it can be fun to envision marriage, avoid serious discussions until marriage is a realistic possibility. You should complete school and be in a position to attain financial stability.

- Another consideration is whether or not your judgment has been tainted by involvement in premarital sex. Girls especially tend to become emotionally connected prematurely when sex is thrown into the mix. It's common for thoughts of marriage to arise when you are already doing as married couples do. So you should be free of sexual involvement before you look seriously at marriage.

- Make sure the feelings are mutual. Girls can become committed more quickly than boys. Just weeks before one boyfriend broke up with me, I was naming our future children. Obviously we were not on the same page.

Question: *Am I called to a religious vocation?*

Linda

STOP! Don't skip this question because you are con-
vinced that a religious vocation is not for you. You can't
confidently exclude this calling without giving it serious
consideration.

In order to be completely content in life, you need to
hide yourself in the heart of God. The best way to arrive at
the center of *his* will is to surrender *your* will. Ask the Lord
what he wants for you. Then trust that he will lead you to
that perfect place.

When we look at the vowed religious life, we tend to
think of sacrifice. The lifelong commitment of religious
to never have sex seems like the greatest sacrifice possible, partly because our sex-driven society assumes that
sex is a right and that it is impossible to live without it.
Religious also surrender the intimacy that a married couple enjoy, the possibility of having children and the freedom to live where and how they choose.

You might think you will avoid sacrifice in the vocation of marriage, but think again. No matter what vocation you choose, life is full of challenges and difficulties.
Along with its great joys comes, at times, the most heart-
wrenching suffering.

Marriage is not a blissful, sex-filled utopia. There
are times when couples must abstain from sex—for
example, when using Natural Family Planning to regu-
late the birth of children, when one of the partners is

sick or when one partner is away in the military or on business. Chris travels all over the country and occasionally is gone for extended periods of time. Thank God, he remains chaste in our times of separation.

Sexual purity is an ongoing battle whether you are married, single or in a religious vocation. Within a few months after our wedding, a friend called to congratulate us. He said something to Chris that has stuck with me all these years: "Isn't marriage great? Yet can you see that the lie from Satan before you are married is that you can't wait to have sex, and the lie after you are married is that it is better with someone else?"

As the *Catechism* says when discussing chastity, "Self-mastery is a long and exacting work. One can never consider it acquired once and for all. It presupposes renewed effort at all stages of life [see Titus 2:1–6]" (*CCC* #2342).

The vocation of marriage includes many other sacrifices. A spouse and children require attention, which often dictates how one's time is spent. I wish I could spend just five minutes after Mass in thanksgiving for the great gift of the Eucharist, but usually I have to quiet a child or break up a fight between siblings or prevent a two-year-old from shredding the hymnal.

Chris has made many sacrifices, large and small, in being married to me. Since I am such a light sleeper, he is not able to listen to music or read in bed, which he did before we were married. I know he would like to spend more of the money he makes on books rather than on diapers and violin lessons. But Chris, being a good father, makes sure that the bills are paid and the needs of the children are met.

Aware as I am of all these sacrifices, is it any wonder that I was shocked and irritated when Chris said to me one day, "Did you know that the consecrated celibate single life is the highest expression of a vocation?"

We had just arrived at the grocery store and had three small children napping in the back of the car. I ran in to pick up a few things, my mind racing as I walked through the aisles. "There is no way being single is more difficult than being married and the mother of seven children. How can this be?"

When I returned to the car, I told Chris about the battle raging in my mind. He said, "Linda, it has nothing to do with which vocation is more difficult. It has to do with the way God made it."

Chris explained that a consecrated celibate is an expression or picture of what we all will be one day in heaven. Therefore, it is a higher calling on earth. The vocation of the religious, whether lived as a priest, brother, sister or consecrated celibate single person, is a heavenly vocation. Give this serious consideration when evaluating the path of your life.

Don't be afraid. God's gifts will enable you to live whatever vocation he has for you. The key is to surrender your will to him, allow him to lead you and then love him completely for the rest of your journey.

THE FINAL AND GREATEST MEMORY MOMENT

Linda

March 30, 1991

I spent the morning *waiting*, shut up in the church's nursery. This was the usual place for the bride-to-be and her party to get ready. I took hours curling my hair, putting on make-up and *waiting* while a friend buttoned those twenty-five tiny buttons that ran down the back of my white satin wedding dress. I had a slight sinus headache, which was frustrating because I wanted the day to be perfect in every way.

Outside the door activity mounted. Chris and his crew of friends straightened each other's ties, the wedding coordinator took care of last-minute details, guests arrived, and in the church hall some helpful ladies arranged the food in preparation for the reception.

At a precise moment I was released from my holding cell and led to the door of the sanctuary, where my father stood *waiting* for me. He was beaming with pride. I took his arm, and the wedding march began. As we walked down the aisle, the moment seemed unreal. Everything around me was hazy. The only person I could clearly see was Chris, standing at the end of the aisle, *waiting*.

My father presented me to the man who had won my heart, and the ceremony commenced. It was beautiful; the songs made both our mothers cry. The words of the ceremony were exactly what we wanted, full of our commitment to Christ and the desire to see our families won for the Lord. I cried through the vows and nearly caught my veil on fire with the unity candle. At the end we kissed, and the onlookers snickered at Chris' awkwardness.

Then came the moment I had been waiting for: We were finally introduced as Mr. and Mrs. Christopher Padgett. Our new identity as husband and wife was official.

As the wedding party processed down the aisle and out the door, Chris reached over and smacked me on the butt. My first reaction was shock, because that had been inappropriate for such a long while. But then I realized that it was OK. We were now married. What an awesome revelation.

As we drove away in the red Toyota covered with white shoe polish and pulling strings of pop cans, we looked at each other and acknowledged that it was all worth the *wait*. God's blessing was on our union, and the adventure had begun. And boy, it has been one great adventure.

EPILOGUE
CHRIS AND LINDA

So what do you think? Are you ticked off? Are you bummed to hear yet another voice telling you to abstain from all that sex stuff?

We hope this book has made a difference in the way you will face tomorrow. And we know that for many of you the reminders in this book will matter. For that we are elated.

But we also know that some readers will have closed this book after reading a few things that made them uncomfortable. And some of you who have endured to the end will figure that we just don't understand your situation. You think, if only they knew how much I love my partner, how the sex I have isn't selfish, how this and how that.

In the end there is really nothing we can say or do to make you live differently. The choice for chastity or promiscuity is yours. Our hope is that you will see, believe and apply new boundaries in your life. We promise that you will experience the fruit of discipline and success in the end.

Whatever happens in your life, keep in mind that God is always there. In his great love and concern, he asks you to choose his path, the one that leads to the most happiness.

Our story is just that—our story. The reason we wanted to share it with you was to encourage those who have abandoned virginity already to realize that chastity can once again be yours. Our experience is a success story. We fell into sin but climbed back out into a pure relationship. Through it all we stayed together.

We were not stronger or more spiritually mature than any of you. We were, however, driven by a deep desire to change.

You need to have that same desire in order for conversion to occur. Pretending you want to change when you don't will not help you. Be honest with yourself and with God. If you like doing something but know it is wrong, acknowledge this in prayer and ask for a new outlook and perspective. God will give you the grace and the ability to achieve victory.

May God be with you all as you continue your journey.

Padgett's Ponderings

The phrase "Cat got your tongue"— who came up with that? What is the likelihood of a cat actually snagging a person's tongue and keeping him from talking? Wouldn't you smack the cat to release yourself from its grip?

It would probably be easier for an ant colony or a few good mice to hold a person's tongue captive. Animals such as cats don't have fingers. A monkey could probably hold your tongue. It would have to be a strong monkey to resist your defenses, though. But I think it's really all a bunch of nonsense.

Question: *Has anyone ever really seen a cat hold someone's tongue? If it came to that, what animal would you want holding your tongue? Who came up with this crazy saying?*

Appendix A

A Quiz

1. When taking out a girl it is important to
    a. open her door when getting in the vehicle
    b. tell her if her breath is bad
    c. make her pay for her own food
    d. tell her parents you are only interested in her body
2. Pregnancy is the only thing you need to worry about if you are sexually active.
    a. True
    b. False
3. The best way to break up is
    a. put an ad in the newspaper
    b. send a note
    c. face-to-face
    d. make an announcement on the intercom at school
4. One way to help remain pure while dating is to dress

_____.

5. When meeting your date's parents you should
    a. tell the mother that she is good-looking
    b. honor their requests regarding curfew
    c. make fun of how their house looks
    d. tell them how great their daughter kisses
6. Real men don't eat caviar.
    a. True
    b. I don't see how this applies.

7. God did *not* create sex for
   a. fun
   b. babies
   c. unity within marriage
   d. self-pleasure

8. Dating is all about me.
   a. True
   b. False

9. French kissing is the same as "greeting with a holy kiss."
   a. True
   b. False

10. The purpose of dating is
   a. getting a lot of sexual experience
   b. finding a future marriage partner
   c. driving your parents crazy
   d. remaining popular

11. It is OK to have premarital sexual intercourse as long as you really love each other.
   a. True
   b. False

12. Which would *not* be an example of an inexpensive date?
   a. playing cards at a park
   b. watching the sunset with a bunch of friends
   c. chartering a boat for a day on the water
   d. making dinner for each other at home

13. The birth control pill is 100 percent effective in preventing pregnancy.
    a. True
    b. False

14. Which is the most effective way to prevent pregnancy and disease?
    a. the pill
    b. condoms
    c. oral sex
    d. abstinence

15. An inexpensive date can be just as successful as one that costs lots of money.
    a. True
    b. False

16. Chris and Linda have all the answers and are the smartest people in the world.
    a. True
    b. True

Appendix B

A Meditative Exercise on
1 Corinthians 13, the "Love Chapter"

1. As you read through the passage, replace the word *love* with the word *Jesus*. Meditate on how each statement was reflected in the character and actions of Christ. He was patient, kind, gentle and so forth.
2. Read it again replacing the word *love* with your name. Meditate on how the statements should and will impact your relationships, not only with that special someone but also with your parents, your friends and even yourself. Are you patient, kind, not envious and so forth?
3. Finally, write out each of these statements regarding love, and think about ways you have received love from your parents, your friends and God. How have you returned that love?
4. Take patience, for example.

> I have seen my mother patiently pray and intercede for me when I was disobeying God's will.
>
> I was patient with my sister when she didn't understand what I was trying to tell her the first time around.

1 Corinthians 13

> If I speak in the tongues of mortals and of angels, but do not have love, I am a noisy gong or a clanging cymbal. And if I have prophetic powers, and understand all mysteries and all knowledge, and

if I have all faith, so as to remove mountains, but do not have love, I am nothing. If I give away all my possessions, and if I hand over my body so that I may boast, but do not have love, I gain nothing.

Love is patient; love is kind; love is not envious or boastful or arrogant or rude. It does not insist on its own way; it is not irritable or resentful; it does not rejoice in wrongdoing, but rejoices in the truth. It bears all things, believes all things, hopes all things, endures all things.

Love never ends. But as for prophecies, they will come to an end; as for tongues, they will cease; as for knowledge, it will come to an end. For we know only in part, and we prophesy only in part; but when the complete comes, the partial will come to an end. When I was a child, I spoke like a child, I thought like a child, I reasoned like a child; when I became an adult, I put an end to childish ways. For now we see in a mirror, dimly, but then we will see face to face. Now I know only in part; then I will know fully, even as I have been fully known. And now faith, hope, and love abide, these three; and the greatest of these is love.

Appendix C

Fun Facts About the Authors

Chris

Favorite book, excluding the Bible: *Anything on the Virgin Mary*

Favorite hobby: *Reading*

Favorite drink: *Coffee*

Favorite color: *Red*

Favorite movie: *Dances with Wolves*

Favorite book in the Bible: *The Gospel of John*

Favorite Bible verse: *"Be still, and know that I am God!*
I am exalted among the nations,
I am exalted in the earth" (Psalm 46:10).

Also, "I appeal to you therefore, brothers and sisters, by the mercies of God, to present your bodies as a living sacrifice, holy and acceptable to God, which is your spiritual worship" (Romans 12:1).

Favorite Bible story: *The parable of the Prodigal Son in Luke 15:11–32 and the story of Joseph in Genesis 37, 39–47*

Favorite quote: *"Preach the Gospel at all times, and when necessary use words" (St. Francis of Assisi).*[1]

Favorite dinner: *Chicken pot pie*

Favorite game: *Tetris*

Favorite band: *The Beatles*

Most hated food: *Brussels sprouts*

Favorite time of day: *Evening*

What do you think about the pnematifore of the symphonic degree minor with a hyperbole causing catastrophic experiences in a way that is fantabulous? *Huh?*

Linda

Favorite book, excluding the Bible: *It depends on when you ask.*

Favorite hobby: *Crafts and reading*

Favorite drink: *Iced coffee*

Favorite color: *Yellow*

Favorite movie: *Anne of Green Gables*

Favorite book in the Bible: *The Gospel of John*

Favorite Bible verse: *"Take delight in the Lord, and he will give you the desires of your heart"* *(Psalm 37:4).*
The story of Hannah and Samuel in 1 Samuel 1–2
"The will of God will never lead you where the grace of God cannot keep you" (Author unknown).

Favorite dinner: *Potluck*

Favorite game: *Solitaire*

Favorite band: *None*

Most hated food: *Yogurt*

What do you think about the pnematifore of the symphonic degree minor with a hyperbole causing catastrophic experiences in a way that is fantabulous? *Oh, stop it, Chris!*

Appendix D

Resources

Contraception

Doyle, Fletcher. *Natural Family Planning Blessed Our Marriage: 19 True Stories.* Cincinnati: Servant, 2006.

Gift Foundation offers information on Natural Family Planning and related topics. Visit http://www.giftfoundation.org.

Kippley, John. *Birth Control and Christian Discipleship.* Cincinnati: Couple to Couple League, 1994.

Kippley, John and Sheila. *The Art of Natural Family Planning.* Cincinnati: Couple to Couple League, 1996.

Kuhar, Bogomir. *Infant Homicides Through Contraceptives,* second ed., Bardstown, Ky.: Eternal Life, 1994.

Smith, Janet. *Contraception: Why Not?* VHS, DVD, pamphlet, transcript and study guide, 1999. Available from One More Soul, 1846 N. Main St., Dayton, OH 45405-3832, 800-307-7685, http.//www.omsoul.com.

Dating

Fields, Doug and Todd Temple. *Creative Dating.* Nashville: Thomas Nelson, 1986.

Harris, Joshua. *I Kissed Dating Goodbye.* Sisters, Ore.: Multnomah, 2003.

NOT READY FOR MARRIAGE, NOT READY FOR SEX

Pregnancy

Birthright can refer you to a pregnancy counseling center in your area. Call 800-848-LOVE.

Catholic Charities, the largest private network of social service organizations in the United States, provides help for women of all faiths who are facing an unexpected pregnancy. Call 800-CARE-002.

Fraser, Becky with Linda Shands. *Stand Up Girl: Take Charge of Your Unexpected Pregnancy.* Cincinnati: Servant, 2005. Also see the Web site www.standupgirl.com.

Project Rachel is a network of professional counselors and priests, all trained to provide one-on-one spiritual and psychological care for those who are suffering because of an abortion. Call 800-5WE-CARE.

Sexuality

Bonacci, Mary Beth. *Real Love.* San Francisco: Ignatius, 1996.

Evert, Jason. *If You Really Loved Me: 100 Questions on Dating, Relationships and Sexual Purity.* San Diego: Catholic Answers, 2003.

_____. *Pure Love.* San Diego: Catholic Answers, 2003.

Healy, Mary. *Men & Women Are from Eden: A Study Guide to John Paul II's Theology of the Body.* Cincinnati: Servant, 2005.

May, William. *Catholic Sexual Ethics.* Huntington, Ind.: Our Sunday Visitor, 1996.

McDowell, Josh and Dick Day. *Why Wait?* San Bernardino: Here's Life, 1987.

Stenzel, Pam. *Sex Ed: No Screwing Around,* faith-based and public school versions, DVD and VHS, available at http://pamstenzel.com.

———. *Sex Has a Price Tag: Discussions about Sexuality, Spirituality and Self-Respect.* Grand Rapids, Mich.: Zondervan, 2003.

West, Christopher. *Good News about Sex and Marriage,* rev. ed. Cincinnati: Servant, 2004.

———. *Theology of the Body Explained: A Commentary on John Paul II's "Gospel of the Body."* Boston: Pauline, 2003.

———. *Theology of the Body for Beginners: A Basic Introduction to Pope John Paul II's Sexual Revolution.* West Chester, Pa.: Ascension, 2004. http://www.theology-ofthebody.com

Spiritual Growth

Pinto, Matthew J. *Did Adam & Eve Have Belly Buttons? And 199 Other Questions from Catholic Teenagers.* West Chester, Pa.: Ascension, 1998.

http://www.motherofallpeoples.com. Click on "Youth Zone."

Notes

Section One: Initial Infatuation

1. Sister Mary Elizabeth, "Venerable Teresita: Her Secret Was Mary," in *From the Housetops*, Vol. XLIV, No. 2, 2004, Still River, Mass.: St. Benedict Center, p. 2.

2. Joshua Harris, *I Kissed Dating Goodbye* (Sisters, Ore.: Multnomah, 1997), p. 191.

3. A. C. Green, quoted in *Practicing Teen Chastity*, a pamphlet from the Foundation for the Family, Cincinnati, and in Jason Evert, *Pure Love* (San Diego: Catholic Answers, 1999), p. 4.

Section Two: The Fall

1. Matthew J. Pinto, *Did Adam & Eve Have Belly Buttons? And 199 Other Questions from Catholic Teenagers* (West Chester, Pa.: Ascension, 1998), p. 209.

2. Tim Stafford, *Worth the Wait* (Grand Rapids, Mich.: Zondervan, 1998), p. 97.

3. Josh McDowell and Dick Day, *Why Wait?* (San Bernardino, Calif.: Here's Life, 1987), p. 200.

4. Stafford, p. 47.

5. Thomas and Donna Finn, *Intimate Bedfellows: Love, Sex, and the Catholic Church* (Boston: Daughters of St. Paul, 1993), p. 35.

Section Three: The Change

1. *From the Housetops*, p.8.
2. *Catholic Teen Survival Guide: Love and Dating*. Agoura Hills, Calif.: Veritas, 2001, p. 16.
3. *Catholic Teen Survival Guide*, p. 16.
4. John R. Diggs, Jr., pamphlet "Are Condoms Better Than Nothing?" (Sioux Falls, S.D.: Abstinence Clearinghouse, 2001).

Section Four: Hard Questions

1. *Catholic Teen Survival Guide*, p. 22.
2. National Institutes of Health, www.niaid.nih.gov.
3. Mary Beth Bonacci, *Real Love* (San Francisco: Ignatius, 1996), p. 71.
4. McDowell and Day, p.101.
5. *Catholic Teen Survival Guide*, p. 8.
6. John R. Diggs, Jr., MD, pamphlet "Human Papilloma Virus" (Sioux Falls, S.D.: Abstinence Clearinghouse, 2001).
7. "What are the Risk Factors for Cervical Cancer?" at www.cancer.org.
8. Cathy Brown, "Teen Pregnancy Decreasing? Not Exactly," *Celebrate Life*, a publication of American Life League, March-April 2001, p. 41.
9. J. C. Wilke, M.D., "Contraceptive Pill," Life Issues Institute, www.lifeissues.org.

10 See Paul Weckenbrock, R.Ph.D., "The Pill: How Does It Work? Is It Safe?" p. 4, at the Web site for Couple to Couple League International, www.ccli.org.

11. 2005 Physicians' Desk Reference (Montvale, N.J.: Thomson Physician Desk Reference, 2005), p. 3338.

12. Brown, p. 40.

13. "Date Rape: A Power Trip," pamphlet from the National Crime Prevention Council, Washington, D.C.

Appendix A

1. This is a popular adaptation of Chapter XVII of Francis' Rule of 1221, in which Francis told the friars not to preach unless they had received the proper permission to do so. Then he added, "Let all the brothers, however, preach by their deeds." See Father Pat McCloskey, o.f.m., "Ask a Franciscan," *St. Anthony Messenger*, www.americancatholic.org.